HOW TO MAKE LOVE
SIX NIGHTS A WEEK

is a guide for those who want to bring
back the thrill they felt when they first
met the man or woman in their life. It's
a guide for those who feel their love
life is pretty good . . . but have the
unsettling feeling that it could be
much, much better. It's a guide for
those who have colorful and exciting
sexual fantasies inside their heads, but
who don't know how to bring those
fantasies to life . . ."

Here is a richly erotic tour through
the world of delicious sex—in the
one book that shows you the way to
ultra-hot lovemaking beyond your
wildest imagination . . . and more
often than you ever dreamed
possible!

HOW TO
MAKE LOVE
SIX NIGHTS
A WEEK

by
Graham Masterton

A SIGNET BOOK

*For Wiescka . . . with thanks
for every single day.*

SIGNET
Published by the Penguin Group
Penguin Books USA Inc., 375 Hudson Street,
New York, New York 10014, U.S.A.
Penguin Books Ltd, 27 Wrights Lane,
London W8 5TZ, England
Penguin Books Australia Ltd, Ringwood,
Victoria, Australia
Penguin Books Canada Ltd, 2801 John Street,
Markham, Ontario, Canada L3R 1B4
Penguin Books (N.Z.) Ltd, 182-190 Wairau Road,
Auckland 10, New Zealand

Penguin Books Ltd, Registered Offices:
Harmondsworth, Middlesex, England

First published by Signet, an imprint of New American Library,
a division of Penguin Books USA Inc.

First Printing, April, 1991
10 9 8 7 6 5 4 3 2 1

Copyright © Graham Masterton, 1991
All rights reserved

 REGISTERED TRADEMARK—MARCA REGISTRADA

Printed in the United States of America

Contents

PROLOGUE

You Can Get It If You Really Want It!

Do you get enough sex?

Enough meaning as much as you want, as often as you want, and as satisfying as you expect it to be?

Traditionally, it's supposed to be men who are always complaining that they never get enough. And it's true, yes, that a lot of men do feel sexually short-changed. The most common complaint is that after several years of marriage—and particularly after the birth of a child—their lovemaking simply peters out.

"She's always too tired." "She just doesn't seem interested." "She doesn't seem to get turned on any more."

But the striking part about it is that just as many *women* feel they're not getting enough.

"These days, he's interested only in his career." "He never tries to seduce me." "He's always too tired, or too drunk, or too stressed."

The fact is that in thousands of marriages and sexual relationships, *both* partners feel that they're not getting sex as often as they would ideally like. They don't always blame their love-partners. Sometimes they appreciate that work or children or other domestic circumstances can temporarily affect their sex lives, and that, for the time being, they have no alternative but to make the best of what they can get.

Yet in most cases, fairly or unfairly, they *do* hold their husband or wife or lover at least partially responsible. And when this happens, it is often a great deal more difficult for them to break out of the deadlock of silent resentment and help their sex life to flourish once more.

But how much sex is enough sex?

You may be surprised to discover that more and more modern sex counselors are beginning to believe that—ideally—you should at least *consider* the possibility of making love every single day; and sometimes more than once a day. Of course it won't always be possible. It's understandably difficult for a man to make love to his wife when he's on a sales trip in Cleveland, and she's back home in New Jersey. Sometimes one partner will have the flu, or a stomach ache, or be genuinely too tired.

But every day when you're together you should both think about expressing your affection for each other sexually, and if at all possible, you should do it.

There are many reasons why the frequency of your lovemaking can start to fall off. In this book, I shall examine those reasons in detail, and see how they can be quickly and effectively overcome. In other words, how you can have sex much more often—six times a week, without any difficulty. And *better* sex, too. Wonderfully better sex.

One of the most common causes of anxiety and frustration is that women often fail to understand the normality of their sexual urges. They have been brought up to believe that there is something wrong in a woman wanting not just regular but frequent sex. The intensity of their sexual fantasies can shock them, too.

"I was ashamed because I thought about sex almost all of the time," said Lois, of Silver Spring, Maryland. "I used to have the dirtiest fantasies you could imagine, and of course I used to think that I was some kind of female pervert.

"When I was waking up in the morning, I used to daydream about five or six men all making love to me at once. Can you imagine that? I had two huge cocks in my mouth, two huge cocks side-by-side in my pussy, and a fifth huge cock up my ass. I wanted them to stretch me, to force me wide open, to shove me and shake me and ram themselves right up into me. Then I wanted them all to come at once, filling up my mouth, filling my pussy, filling my ass.

"This fantasy used to make me so wet and excited that I was ready to make love to Robert right then and there; but he always used to get out of bed around six o'clock to go to work; and even on weekends he used to get up early. So he was never there to take advantage of the way I felt.

"Because I was so frustrated I used to spend the rest of the day thinking about sex. I would have done absolutely anything for a good couple of hours in bed with Robert. I used to masturbate on and off for most of the day, either with my fingers, by tugging my panties up between my legs, or occasionally by using a shampoo bottle. Once I carved two huge carrots into the shape of cocks and lay stark naked on the livingroom rug and masturbated with them all afternoon. In the end I secretly bought a vibrator and used that. I used to call it 'Henry,' would you believe?

"I really began to think that I was mentally sick. It was only after I read one of your books that I realized that plenty of other women have sexual urges that are just as strong as mine and that they're completely natural. The fault was partly Robert's because he didn't understand that a woman could need sex so much; and partly mine, because I was ashamed of the way I felt and didn't tell him.''

Lois was lucky. After reading *How To Drive Your Man Wild In Bed* she was able to pluck up the confidence to explain to her husband how she felt, and he was not only understanding but aroused. In the last letter she sent me, she confessed that she still occasionally masturbates during the day, but only because she likes it, not because she needs to. She and Robert now make the time to have sex four or five times a week, and 'Henry' has definitely been demoted to second fiddle.

When a relationship is subjected to any kind of stress, lovemaking invariably suffers first. The stress may have its origins in money, or career complications, or the problems of drink or drugs. Sometimes the stress can be caused by quite minor problems, such as tension about a forthcoming social event. But the effects on your sex life can be profound and long-lasting, and I have come across several relationships in which comparatively insignificant problems have been allowed to cut deep to the core of the couple's sexual happiness.

The point is that both men and women do need frequent sex in a sexual relationship, and that it is neither shameful nor unusual to want to make love every day of the week. Another point to remember is that while your fantasies may seem extreme, you can actually be satisfied by quite straightforward lovemaking. In other words, while Lois might have fantasized about making love to several men several times, she was sexually quite satisfied with Robert making love to her just once.

Nor need you think that every act of love in a frequent-sex relationship has to qualify for an

Earth-Moved Medal. It is not the Richter scale of your climaxes that you need to worry about—or even having a climax at all. It's simply the fact of getting close together and sharing each other's bodies. Of kissing, and caressing, and opening yourself physically and mentally to somebody who really cares about you. The closer a couple can be between the sheets, the closer they can be at all times.

Frequent sexual intimacy is a good habit to get into, but sometimes you have to work at it because it's a habit that's very easy to get out of; and *very* difficult to get back into again.

Mary-Jane, a homemaker from Fort Wayne, Indiana, wrote and asked what she could do to arouse a husband who went to bed every single night in his pajamas with a good book which he would assiduously read until it was time for him to turn over and go to sleep. By their nature, men are always susceptible to getting themselves stuck into a routine, and Mary-Jane's husband had gotten himself stuck into a routine that didn't include making love to Mary-Jane.

What she had to do was to re-introduce the idea of regular sex into their relationship. The way she did this was to slide her hand into his pajamas every time he settled down to read his book, and massage his penis. When he stiffened, she then kissed and sucked and rubbed him to a climax. She did this *every single night* until the idea of having a regular ejaculation became something that he expected. More and more often the book was set aside and Mary-Jane's caresses were rewarded with intercourse.

The reason I suggested to Mary-Jane that she use this technique was because it placed no sexual demands on her husband whatsoever, and it involved no conversation that might have become argumentative and made an awkward marital situation worse. Also, it gave her regular practice in caressing and stimulating her husband's penis, which is something which many women—even women who have been married for many years—still do shyly or awkwardly.

"I wasn't very good at it to begin with. I was too hurried and rough. But I began to learn what kind of strokes he liked . . . long and slow, tugging the skin slightly with each downstroke, and circling around and around the opening of his cock with the ball of my thumb, especially when it started to get a little slippery.

"I learned to be better at kissing him, too. Taking my time, making sure that I enjoyed myself just as much as him. I like holding his cock in my hand and running the tip of my tongue all the way around the head of it, and then pushing the tip of my tongue into the opening, just the tip, so that he can watch me doing it."

Mary-Jane became adept, too, at anal stimulation, sliding her index finger into her husband's anus as he came close to a climax, and using a beckoning motion to intensify his ejaculation.

Her verdict after only three weeks: "We make love so often now that I literally lose count, and it's so much more exciting."

Initiating sex without words is often a help in relationships where lovemaking has become infrequent. Here, for example, is how thirty-three-year-old Sharon, a beautician from Waldwick, New Jersey, tried (and failed) to rekindle her husband's sexual interest.

"We hadn't made love for three or four weeks. I was feeling so frustrated. I kept trying to act all smoochy and seductive but somehow Ray just didn't seem to get the message. In the end I really made myself over—highlighted my hair, polished my nails, and bought myself a slinky black negligee. When he came home from work I lay back on the couch and called, 'Hi, darling, why don't you come and make love to me?'

"He took it all the wrong way. He seemed to think that I was trying to suggest that he wasn't any good at sex. What was supposed to be a seductive evening ended up as a shouting-match. It was terrible. I felt like a whore . . . and not a very successful whore, at that."

What had gone wrong? Well, although Sharon had taken the constructive step of initiating a sexual situation, it was a sexual situation which still obliged Ray to show some positive action. He had to undress, he had to lie Sharon down on the couch or the floor or take her to bed. Since he was out of the habit of making love to her, it was therefore easier for him to reject her advances than have to demonstrate that he was prepared to respond.

As it turned out, Ray had been worried about work, and his anxiety had caused temporary impotence. He was the kind of man who was very sensitive about any inability to have an erection; and so he had stopped making love to Sharon rather than risk her ridicule.

Psychologically-caused impotence has the insidious characteristic of feeding on itself. The more fearful a man is that he might not be able to have an erection, the less likely he is to be able to have one.

So, no matter how provocative Sharon made herself, she was not going to be able to stir up any kind of sexual response with a scenario which required Ray to take down his pants and brandish a huge erection. Instead, Ray felt even more resentful, even more stressed, and ended up believing that he was a failure at home as well as at work.

If Sharon had used a technique similar to Mary-Anne's—gently and regularly massaging Ray's penis when they were in bed together—and *showing no frustration or disappointment if he failed to produce an erection*—then she would have been well on the road to restoring frequent and zestful intercourse. In fact, she and Ray ended up seperating for several months, and only after Ray had undergone sexual counseling were they able to get back together again.

Many women feel that when it comes to sex, the man in their life should be in charge. It's a man's duty to know all about sex and to apply that knowledge in a masterful way. All a woman should have to do is lie back and think of what to have for dinner tomorrow.

Women write to me with all kinds of complaints about their partners' sexual performance. When I first suggest that they could do something positive themselves to improve their love lives, their initial reaction is nearly always, "Why me? *He's* the one who's supposed to be in charge!"

They refuse to contemplate (a) that their partners' sexual shortcomings might partially be rooted in their own apparent lack of sexual response; or that (b) it's their job to do anything about it. "If he's not making love to me often enough, that's *his* fault, not mine!"

When it comes to sex, however, there are no trades unions; and no job demarcation. Whoever is in the better position to initiate improvements in a sexual relationship, it is up to him (or her) to take steps to do so—regardless of whose "fault" the problems might appear to be.

A major part of taking those steps is for you both

to identify how often you feel you need sex and the level of your day-to-day sexuality. That's why I've prepared a questionnaire at the end of this chapter which both you and your partner can fill out to check exactly how strong your sexual interest is and how often you should ideally be making love. By "making love," I am including any erotic act that you and your partner do together, from simply caressing each other sexually to full intercourse.

This questionnaire is emphatically *not* designed to give you a hard-and-fast Sexuality Quotient. In other words, it won't tell you how sexy you are in comparison with the population at large. But if you and your partner both complete it, it will allow you to judge whether he needs sex much more frequently than you, or if you you need sex much more frequently than him . . . or if you both need approximately the same amount of sex.

There can be huge variations in your sexual needs, and it isn't uncommon for a woman who is very sexually active to find herself in a relationship with a man for whom once a month would be more than enough. Or, of course, the other way around.

There is absolutely nothing wrong with a woman wanting sex almost all the time; any more than there is anything wrong with a woman who feels the need to make love only very infrequently. The key to sexual success with your partner lies in understanding what he wants, making sure that he understands what *you* want, and taking the necessary steps to make sure that both of you are sexually fulfilled in the way which excites and satisfies you the most.

That is the purpose of the questionnaire . . . to see how closely your sexual number matches that of your partner so that (if necessary) both of you can then take action to redress the balance.

There are many stimulating ways in which a partner who *doesn't* feel the urge to have sex very often can satisfy a partner who does, with the minimum of sexual participation on his or her own part. Laura, a thirty-eight-year-old legal secretary from Detroit, found that her marriage became "far more balanced and much less aggressive" when she encouraged her husband George to watch sex videos and read explicit sex magazines. "Personally, I've never been a tremendously sexual person, but George could happily have sex morning, noon and night. Once I understood that there was nothing *wrong* with him, that he wasn't a dirty old satyr but simply a man with a very high interest in physical sex, I began to straighten our marriage out. He watches sex videos while we're in bed together, while I catch up with my law studies. The only thing I have to do is to use one hand to massage his cock.

"To tell you the truth, I often get turned on myself, and what starts as a massage ends up as lovemaking. Since I started encouraging George to watch his videos and read his magazines I probably have intercourse twice as frequently as I ever did before. That's more than enough for me, but it's done wonders for our marriage. We're so much more relaxed and friendly together than we ever used to be.

"Yes, absolutely, I like the way our sex life has turned out. I'm not jealous of the girls in the videos or the magazines . . . no woman should be. In fact I see them as my friends because *they're* doing the job of turning on my husband when I don't particularly feel like it.

"Naturally enough, George enjoys a little participation on my part when he's actually climaxing, but he doesn't insist on it. Usually, when he climaxes I massage his cock with his own sperm until he goes soft again. Sometimes he leans across the pillow when he's about to climax, and shoots his sperm over my breasts. Lately, when I've felt in the mood, I've taken his cock between my lips, and let him shoot his sperm into my mouth. I didn't use to like that at first, but I saw so many girls on George's videos doing it that I decided to try it. I quite enjoy the taste of it now, it's kind of sweet and salty at the same time; and I know George gets a great deal of pleasure out of my doing it."

That was how a woman who didn't care too much for sex ended up with a much more rewarding marriage and a sex life that satisfied both herself and her husband. Agreed: Laura had to make a considerable change of attitude toward sex videos and magazines—and agreed: she often has to massage George when she may be more interested in reading or studying. But the practical truth of the matter is that it is almost always the less-sexual partner who holds the answer to improving the relationship. Only you can judge whether the compromises that you have to make are worth the reward.

What happens when a woman is considerably more interested in sex than the man in her life?

She may often feel guilty and ashamed and prefer *not* to tell her partner that she is sexually frustrated. After the publication of my previous book *Sex Secrets of the Other Woman*, I received a desperate letter from Sherri, of Cedar Rapids, Iowa, complaining that "I'm not at all worried about satisfying my boyfriend. What I'm worried about is that he doesn't seem to satisfy *me*.

"You keep giving women good advice about how to deal with a man's insatiable sex drive. Well, compared to my sex drive, my boyfriend's is more of a sex stroll. He doesn't seem to mind if he doesn't have sex for weeks on end while I feel like it every single day. In fact, I need it three or four times a week, every week, or else I start to go crazy. Please don't say that I'm a nymphomaniac. I don't think I am."

Laura was quite right. She wasn't a nymphomaniac. Although "nymphomaniac" is colloquially used to describe any woman who shows a conspicuous interest in men, its clinical definition is a woman who can never be sexually satisfied, no matter how frequently or how furiously she makes love.

Just because a woman is dissatisfied with her sex life—just because she feels that her lover isn't making love to her frequently enough—doesn't make her a nymphomaniac. That simply makes her just the same as sixty-seven percent of all the women I've interviewed in twenty years of sex counseling.

"Nymphomaniac" is a word which men wrongly use to describe women who have a keener sexual appetite than they do. And believe me, a whole lot of women do.

Laura *could* be sexually satisfied. But her problem was that she *wasn't* being sexually satisfied. Her boyfriend simply didn't make love to her often enough.

"I simply don't know what to do. He shows no interest in ever 'having an early night.' And when I try to talk about sex, he changes the subject, or accuses me of 'talking dirty.' He seems to prefer a late-night movie to a late-night lovemaking session. I don't know why he didn't marry the television."

Again and again, I hear the same lament. The boyfriend who seemed so eager to get inside her panties when they were courting has now become the husband who shows scarcely any interest in sex. He's settled down to a dull routine of work, television, bed and breakfast; and sex has become an extra-curricular chore.

Laura said, "I always fantasized that when we got married, we would make love practically all the time. I mean that's the sexy part about marriage to me, that you can have sex of any kind whenever you want."

It always strikes me as ironic that there are so many men who are desperate for a sexual relationship—men whose only sexual satisfaction is a copy of *Penthouse* and their own hand—while so many women in so many marriages are absolutely aching for more sex.

Laura wrote about her husband, "When he came home from the office one evening last month, I opened the door naked except for a twisted hippie-style headband, which he used to love, and several bracelets. He took one look at me and said, 'You took your shower early,' and walked straight past me. And this man is only thirty-three years old! What's he going to be like when he's forty? Or fifty? Or beyond?"

The answer is that her husband is going to become steadily less and less interested in having sex with her, until they have virtually no sex life at all. I see this pattern being repeated over and over. The intense courtship, the honeymoon, the first few months of sexual excitement. Then the frequency of lovemaking gradually decreases until the couple scarcely ever make love at all.

The results are increased tension, a sense of disenchantment and frustration, and quite often the development of a feverishly obsessive interest in sex by one or both partners. The trouble is, this obsessive interest finds its outlet in lone sexual activity, carried out furtively, rather than in shared lovemaking.

While self-stimulation is not physically or mentally harmful in any way, it can have the effect of eroding the erotic need which one partner feels for the other and making it less likely that the urgency of sheer sexual need will bring them closer together again.

This is John, a thirty-four-year-old civil engineer from Baltimore: "Less than a year after we started living together, Clara seemed to lose almost all of her sex-drive. She kept our apartment beautifully clean, she could cook like an angel, she could organize dinner-parties that people practically used to fight to get themselves invited to. But when it came to bedtime, she cleaned off her makeup and climbed into bed and that was it. A peck on the cheek, lights out, sleep tight.

"I loved her, and she turned me on. But I started to masturbate out of total frustration. I never told her that I did it. I started buying porno magazines pretty regularly and masturbated whenever she came home late from seeing her sister, which was two or three times a week. I used to strip naked and stand in front of the mirror and slowly pull myself off, with a whole lot of magazines spread all around me, opened up to my favorite pictures. I used to like shooting my load all over the pictures— that turned me on the most; or sometimes I'd finish off by pressing my cock up against the cold glass of the mirror and shooting all over my stomach.

"The trouble was, masturbation was never as satisfying as lovemaking, and I always felt ashamed of myself after I'd done it. I'd throw all these sperm-filled magazines away and tell myself that I would never masturbate again. But after a couple of days I used to crave the magazines again and regret that I'd gotten rid of them."

As I have said, there is absolutely nothing wrong with masturbation *per se*. It's probably the only really pleasurable human activity that carries no health risk. But because John was seeking relief on his own, that meant that his physical need for Clara was diminished; a diminution which she rapidly sensed, and to which she responded by becoming even more houseproud and even less interested in sex.

As a matter of fact, Clara's behavior was characteristic of many women who live together with men rather than marrying them. Their heightened interest in home-making comes from a sense of insecurity; and what appears to be a lowered interest in sex comes from their need to have constant proof that their lover is prepared to conquer and re-conquer them every time they make love. The problem is that many men mistake their lover's need to be conquered for sexual disinterest, and quickly give up trying.

Men are rarely as sexually confident as they like to appear, and if they encounter too much resistance, they can soon lose faith in their attractiveness and their ability to arouse you. Also, it's difficult for a man to sustain a viable erection when he's worrying too much about having to win you over.

Once a man finds it easier not to try, the couple rapidly get out of the habit of having frequent sex, and it's off down the slippery slope to a relationship where nightly sex is the exception rather than the rule.

In John's case, his problem was gradually solved by showing Clara a great deal of sexual interest and attention, even when she rebuffed him. If he ever felt grievously frustrated when he was in bed with her, I recommended that he should masturbate . . . not secretly, but quite openly, constantly encouraging her participation by guiding her hand around his penis, showing her how he was stroking it; and by making sure that he climaxed over her hand or her thigh or between her legs. In other words, he had to demonstrate graphically how much he wanted her and how much she turned him on.

Kay became obsessive about sex, too, when her husband's new responsibilities at work started to bring him home later and tire him out more. "There was one whole month when we didn't touch each other once," said twenty-eight-year-old Kay, who was employed as a doctor's receptionist in Seattle. "After more than a year, I took to masturbation. It started off very occasionally, slipping my hand into my panties and feeling my clitoris. Then I started using a vaginal syringe that my mother had bought for me when Martin and I first got married. She always had old-fashioned ideas about being clean inside and out. I used to fill the bulb with warm water and take it into the shower with me. I liked to kneel on the floor of the shower-stall with the water splashing over me, and slide the syringe in and out, while I quickly flicked at my clitoris with my fingertips. The look of it used to turn me on. The syringe was shiny black rubber, quite thin and hard, like you'd imagine an animal's penis to be. I used to bend forward so that I could watch it sliding in and out of me. Shiny black rubber, shiny pink flesh.

"I took to pushing it into my bottom, too. I lay on my back in the shower with my legs stretched wide apart and my heels braced against the tiles. Then I would slowly push the syringe into my bottom until it was right inside me, right up to the bulb. It made a tight, squeaky, rubbery noise, and the cold stiff feeling of it right up my bottom always made me shudder. I would push it in and out, deliberately doing it slowly at first to tantalize myself, but then doing it more quickly and forcefully, until

I was sore, but an exciting soreness. I used to masturbate myself with my other hand. Ever since I was a young girl I've had this way of masturbating where I open up the lips of my vagina as far as I can with my index finger and my ring finger, and flick my clitoris quickly with my middle finger.

"When I was near to an orgasm, I used to push the syringe deep into my bottom, and squeeze the bulb so that I was suddenly flooded with warm water. I used to have an orgasm almost at once, and I used to pull out the syringe, so that the water would come jetting out of my bottom like a fountain."

Because she worked for a medic, Kay came across catalogs for all kinds of enema equipment, and she ordered and bought a whole variety of douches and syringes. What had started as a means of seeking sexual satisfaction in a lackluster marriage became an erotic obsession, and she would masturbate two or even three times a day. "I subscribed to *Water & Power* magazine and carried it home hidden in my pocketbook. It was full of articles on enemas, and I used to read it and have fantasies about Martin discovering me on my hands and knees in the shower-stall, with the clyster up inside me."

Kay became so wrapped up in her sexual self-stimulation that even her workaholic husband began to notice the change in her. He wrote me a letter saying that she was becoming "sexually distant," and it was only when I eventually managed to talk to her that the whole story came out. To begin with, Martin was deeply shaken by what she had been doing, and especially the fact that she had been doing it without his knowledge.

"I feel like I've been cuckolded . . . but by what? A rubber syringe!"

When I explained to him that Kay's behavior was completely comprehensible, considering how much she craved sexual fulfillment and how sexually disinterested he had appeared to be, he began to understand. He also understood that Kay had returned to a sexual activity that conjured up both the security and the erotic naughtiness of childhood. Kay's very first memories of sexual pleasure had come from her mother's habit of giving her both vaginal douches and anal enemas, and when Martin let her down, that was the feeling she wanted to recreate.

Their relationship was dramatically improved by Martin being included in Kay's sexual secret. Said Kay: "When it all came out into the open, Martin was pretty shocked and bewildered at first, but when I told him how much I loved him, and that I was doing it only because I wasn't getting enough of him, he began to get over it. The real breakthrough came when I asked Martin to come into the shower with me and watch what I did. He knelt down next to me while I pushed the syringe in and out of my bottom, and then I let him do it. He said he had never realized that I could open my legs so wide. I masturbated with my fingers, tugging my vaginal lips as far apart as I could, and showing Martin how I flicked at my clitoris. He reached over and slid his finger into my open vagina, as well as working away with the syringe, really hard, so that I was wincing with every stroke. When I was ready to climax, I told Martin to squeeze the douche, which he did. The feeling of water filling my insides up was incredible. I knew that I was going to have a huge orgasm, but I wanted Martin inside me, too. Martin climbed over me, and I grasped his penis in my hand. The head of it was crimson, and really swollen. I pressed it against my vagina, and then I buried it right inside me. That feeling was just too much. I released all of the water that was in my bottom, and it spurted over Martin's balls. He climaxed too, and I remember him shouting out, and great hot loops of white come flying around in the shower and spattering across my breasts."

Kay's sexual relationship with Martin began to improve from that moment on. After a while, as their lovemaking increased in frequency and intensity, the infantile excitement which she associated with enemas began to mean less and less to her, and now she uses the syringe "scarcely ever." Their sex has broadened and matured, although they still both see that totally uninhibited act of love in the shower as the starting-point of their revived relationship.

Martin says, "If you can both show each other what your sexual needs are without any kind of fear of shock or disapproval, then you're well on your way to a fantastic sex life. To be able to say to your lover, I'd like to try this or that, without being worried that they're going to say that you're crude and disgusting, that's what it's all about. It doesn't mean they have to like it, or even try it. But it's getting the thought out into the open, sharing it with somebody, that takes all the frustration out of it."

I deliberately chose quite an extreme case to illustrate that all women have strong sexual needs, and some have very strong sexual needs. Kay's case is a classic example of a woman who felt unable to articulate her needs and who almost lost her marriage because of it. Martin's sex drive was by no means as strong as hers, but once he had recognized what Kay wanted, he started to make a particular and regular effort to keep her satisfied.

Again you can see from Kay's and Martin's experience that the less sexually-motivated partner (Martin) was the one who had to make a positive contribution to their sexual relationship in order to save it.

Once you have determined which of you is the more sexually driven, you and your partner can make many exciting and pleasurable adjustments to your relationship so that *both* of you are sexually satisfied.

It quite often happens that love-partners are fairly equally matched as far as their sexual appetites are concerned, but that their sexual clocks are way out of kilter. She likes making love in the morning; he prefers it in the evening. He wakes up in the small hours with a huge erection and wants to have intercourse instantaneously; she wants to lie on the couch after dinner and be slowly seduced (just when he wants to close his eyes and have a nap!)

Here's a couple who found a way around their sexual clock problem by making a simple pact. They agreed to *never* refuse one another, even if their participation was not always wildly enthusiastic.

Don, a thirty-three-year-old auto salesman from San Diego, is a 2 A.M. stallion.

"I work hard all day, I come home, I watch a little TV, maybe I have a couple of beers. By that time I'm totally out of it. All I want to do is to sleep. So I take a shower, go to bed. But by 2 or 3 o'clock, I'm awake, and I've got this raging hard-on, and believe me, nothing short of fucking is going to make this hard-on go away. Sometimes I used to stay awake until morning, with this huge nightstick rearing up between my legs, and the only way I could get it to go down again was to jerk off.

"The trouble was, Maria's completely different.

She's always dressed-up pretty when I get home, there's a nice dinner on the table. She's wearing perfume and lipstick and I know what she wants. She wants me to be smooth and charming, pick her up in my arms and take her to bed then and there. But I could never do that, I was always too dopey. So in the end it got to the point when we just weren't scarcely ever doing it, except on the weekend.

"That was a real bad period in our marriage. One time I was sure we were going to bust up, it got so bad. I felt horny at night and wrecked in the day, and Maria was just as bad, always snapping and nagging."

Eventually, Maria read a copy of *How To Drive Your Man Wild In Bed* and wrote to me. My suggestion was that they should make a pact that would last for at least a month. They should agree to make love whenever one of them wanted to, no arguments, no protestations. Don should sweep Maria off her feet and into bed whenever he came home from work, no matter how exhausted he felt; and Maria should willingly open her legs for Don in the middle of the night, no matter how sleepy she was.

To begin with, both of them were dubious. Don said, "The first night I came home and Maria was dressed up extra-special. She wore this little red mini-dress I always liked, and her gold necklaces, and she was all warpaint and perfume. Me—I'd spent all day taking delivery of fifteen new Dodge Dynastys—and then the traffic on the freeway was backed up for miles. I was tired and I was tense and believe me, the last thing I felt like was fucking.

"But, a deal was a deal, and I carried her to the bedroom, and I unfastened her dress, and I kissed her the way I used to kiss her when we first went out together, and I told her how much I loved her—

which is true, I do. Maybe I just hadn't been saying it often enough. She wore this real pretty little white lacy G-string with bows and pearls sewn on it, and no bra, and she looked cute and sexy, no doubt about it. It's incredible how you can live with somebody and kind of forget to look at them—forget to see how sexy they are.

"I laid her down on the bed and kissed her. Then I stroked her breasts, and kissed her nipples. I spent a whole lot of time kissing her breasts, rolling her nipples in between my fingers, sucking them hard against the roof of my mouth. I hadn't lavished that much attention on her breasts for months, and I'd forgotten how much she enjoyed it, how much it turned her on.

"I guess it relaxed me, too, because I started to get real horny. Maria unbuckled my belt and opened my pants and took out my cock, and started to rub it up and down. I wasn't in a raging rush to make love to her, and because of that, it was a whole lot better. I went down on her, and ran my tongue around the elastic of her G-string. Her pussy was real juicy, but I didn't take her G-string off, I just pulled it to one side, and licked her clit, and then I pushed my tongue right up inside her.

"She was really going, and so was I. I'd forgotten all about the car delivery and the freeway traffic. I climbed on top of her, and she took hold of my cock in her hand and guided it into her pussy. Then she took hold of the cheeks of my ass, and gripped them tight with those sharp fingernails of hers, and so help me, she pulled me right up into her, right up to the balls.

"We didn't do anything out of the ordinary, we just fucked like people normally fuck. But it was beautiful, totally beautiful, and when I went over the top I felt like I was slowly blowing up, you know what I mean, like a slow-motion explosion in the movies. Maria didn't come right away, but after I was finished I went down on her again, and licked her clit, and pushed my tongue right up into her hole, which was totally filled to the brim with pussy-juice and jism, all mingled up. That was when she climaxed, right in my face. She shook and she gasped and she shook and she gasped, and it was just great.

"I guess I slept for a while after that, because the next thing I knew she was kissing the back of my neck and telling me it was time for dinner."

Maria said, "I wasn't too happy about the idea about being woken up in the middle of the night. I can never get back to sleep too easy. But we'd agreed to try it out, you know, and Don had already fulfilled his side of the bargain, so what could I do? Besides, I didn't really have to do too much except lie back and enjoy it. Least, that's what I thought.

"As a matter of fact it didn't work out that way at all. About two o'clock in the morning I woke up and *I* was the one who was feeling horny. Mind you, Don didn't need much encouragement. I just reached out and started stroking his cock, and he went stiff immediately.

"What was terrific about it, though, was that there wasn't the same—what do you call it?—there wasn't the same *need*, there wasn't the same *urgency*. I felt he was doing it because he wanted to do it, and not because he was physically desperate or because he felt he *had* to.

"We made love very, v–e–r–y slowly. I lay back, and Don climbed on top of me, and he slid himself into me like we were always made for each other. Perfect fit. Up and down, up and down, and every time he did it, his cock seemed to feel bigger and to rub me just that little bit more.

"You may not believe this, but up until last night, I had never had an orgasm while we were making love . . . not just from intercourse alone. Don had made me come by going down on me, licking me, and by rubbing me with his fingers. But that was the very first time I reached an orgasm just by intercourse.

"It wasn't the kind of orgasm where you see fireworks and waterfalls and all that stuff. But it gave me a deep, deep kind of satisfaction that I'd never felt before. It kind of washed over me like a wave breaking over a seashore, all the way from my pussy to my brain, and back again, and then back again.

"We kept up the agreement for a few days and then we realized that we didn't have to keep it up any more. We'd fallen in love with each other, maybe for the first time, if I'm going to be truthful. After that, we didn't have to worry about agreements. We just made love day and night, four or five times a week, sometimes more, in the evening, or in the middle of the night, or whenever."

Maria's most fascinating remark is that *"we'd fallen in love with each other, maybe for the first time."*

Again and again, I come across couples who decided to marry or to live together because they *thought* they loved each other, but whose commitment to each other is in fact based on almost everything except love. They got together because they were momentarily infatuated; or because they were rebounding from some other lover; or because they were trying to get away from home; or because they were lonely; or lacking in confidence; or because they needed security.

After several months of living together, a high proportion of these couples begin to feel dissatisfied . . . often without understanding why. But the simple fact is that they have never understood what it is to love somebody—the responsibilities as well as the pleasures. In particular, few of them realize that a satisfying, long-term sexual relationship requires thought, compromise, imagination, caring and constructive effort.

Bringing these qualities to your relationship isn't such hard work as it sounds. But if you want to enjoy the full potential that active sex can bring you, neither you nor your partner can afford to let your lovemaking become no more interesting or exciting than any other domestic chore. A thirty-three-year-old homemaker from Crete, Illinois, told me that "on the whole, I get more of a kick out of baking than I do out of lovemaking."

How To Make Love Six Days A Week isn't a book for beginners, although in it you will find everything you need to know about your body and your sexual psychology for the purposes of stimulating and satisfying lovemaking.

It's a guide for those who want to bring back the tingle that they felt when they first met the man or the woman in their life. It's a guide for those who feel that their love-life is pretty good . . . but have the unsettling feeling that it could be very much better. It's a guide for those who have colorful and exciting sexual fantasies inside of their heads, but don't know how they can bring these fantasies to life.

Some of what you read here you may find shocking. This isn't a guide for prudes. But it observes the strict rule of satisfying sex that I have applied through twenty years of sexual counseling: *Whatever it is—if you're both excited by it, if it gives pleasure to both of you, if it's done without coercion either explicit or implied, if it causes no physical harm, then by all means do it, and enjoy it.*

Because, mostly, this is not so much a guide to sexual stimulation and sexual expertise, but a practical handbook to falling genuinely and deeply in love, and to deriving from your sexual relationship that ultimate joy and fulfillment that can only be described as exaltation.

HOW OFTEN DO YOU NEED SEX?

Both you and your partner should answer all questions. Score 2 for YES, score 1 for NOT SURE, score 0 for NO.

1) Do you think that you would be satisfied if you had sex no more than once a week?

2) Do you think that there is too much emphasis placed on sex on television and in the newspapers?

3) Would you expect the frequency of your love-making to decrease after several years of living together?

4) Do you find your partner less sexually exciting now than when you first met?

5) Do you believe that sexual fantasies are best left as fantasies and that it is wrong to try to play them out?

6) Is oral sex something that you would prefer not to do?

7) Do you find it embarrassing to walk around naked in front of your partner?

8) Do you find it embarrassing to look at your partner when he or she is naked?

9) Is it unnecessarily intimate for partners to scrutinize each other's sex organs closely?

10) Would you be disturbed if your partner wanted to make photographs or videos of you in the nude or making love?

11) Do you feel disconcerted by anything apart from "normal" intercourse?

12) Do you think it is demeaning for a woman to dress erotically to arouse her partner?

13) Does your partner have any sexual appetite which you know about but which you refuse to satisfy?

14) Do you have any sexual appetite which you are too shy to tell your partner about?

15) Do you find the idea of making love anywhere apart from bed to be unappealing?

16) Do you think it is your partner's responsibility to satisfy you sexually?

17) Is it wrong for one partner to try and stimulate the other sexually when he or she obviously doesn't feel like lovemaking?

18A) (for women) Would you be upset if you discovered that your partner had made love to you while you were asleep?

18B) (for men) Do you consider that it would be wrong for you to have intercourse with your partner while she was sleeping?

19) Do you think that couples who want to make love six times a week are oversexed?

20) Do you think that your partner is oversexed?

21) Do you consider it necessary for sexual satisfaction to have a climax every time you make love?

22) Do you find it difficult to talk about your sexual desires with your partner?

23) Do you occasionally wish that it wasn't necessary for you to have sex with your partner?

24) Is there any physical aspect of your partner that you find unappealing?

25) Do you think that strong physical attraction is not strictly necessary in a marriage or long-term relationship?

26) Do you think that pornographic pictures or videos are repulsive?

27) Have you ever pretended that you were too tired or too ill to make love when in fact you simply didn't feel like it?

28) Do you think it would be selfish of your partner to expect you to stimulate him or her even though you didn't want to make love?

29) Are you ashamed of your sexual fantasies?

30) Do you ever wish that you could spend some of your nights alone?

If you scored 0, then you are a well-balanced, sexually-open individual whose love life has limitless potential.

If you scored from 1—15, you have a healthy and constructive attitude toward sex and lovemaking, although there is room for you to be a little less guarded with your partner about some of your sexual preferences.

If you scored between 16—30, you have rather conservative views about sex, and you are cautious and often embarrassed about sexual experimentation. You enjoy lovemaking, but you shy away from any acts that you consider unusual.

If you scored between 31—45, then sexual activity with your partner doesn't rate particularly highly in your relationship, and you would usually place other qualities such as friendship and common leisure pursuits higher on your list of reasons for staying together than sex. You tolerate lovemaking rather than actively participate.

If you scored between 46—60, your sex life is seriously in need of some rethinking and rejuvenation, although even with a score of 60, there is plenty of hope for you yet! It is possible to overcome these anxieties and hang-ups. It is possible to revive the sexual excitement in your relationship even when you thought it was dead and buried.

For the record, compare the figure that you scored with the figure your partner scored. The nearer the two figures are together, the easier it will be for you to re-balance your sexual relationship until you are as near-perfect a pair of lovers as it is possible to find. For instance, if your partner scored 17 and you scored 22, then you have only 5 points of conflicting sexual interest to iron out.

However, even if you scored 0 and your partner scored 60, there is a whole range of sexual inhibition for you to bridge. But it can still be done, and you can start doing it tonight.

1

How Often Is Often Enough?

"I used to feel ashamed of myself because I felt like sex almost all the time." That was how twenty-two-year-old Cindy from Charleston, South Carolina, described the strength of her sexual needs. But of course she had nothing to be ashamed of.

One more-than-important way in which humans differ from animals is that we can feel the urge to have sex at any time, in any season. There's nothing physically or mentally wrong with you if you feel like making love ninety-nine times a day.

It's only when one partner feels like making love a whole lot more often than the other that sexual problems begin to crop up.

Cindy, a checkout girl for a large supermarket, said, "Sometimes it was like a burning, an itch that I couldn't scratch. I used to sit at the checkout thinking about nothing else but what I was going to do with my boyfriend when I got home that evening. I was going to take him straight to bed and make love to him until he begged for mercy.

"I used to think about him all the time, and sometimes I used to go to the bathroom during my break and sit on the john and just stroke my pussy with my fingers, thinking about him.

"There'd be whole weeks when I didn't think about making love at all, but then I'd go through a phase when it was like I was in heat, and I couldn't think about anything else."

Cindy's problem was that her boyfriend Harold—although he was loving and affectionate—didn't have sexual urges of the same high intensity.

The truth is that there are hardly any sexual relationships in which both partners want to make love as often as each other, in the same way as each other, and at the same time of day as each other. You want to make love in the morning. He wants to make love in the evening. There is almost always a percentage of discontent (a percentage which you and your partner can measure with some accuracy by completing the questionnaire at the end of the Introduction).

As I already mentioned, traditional thinking has it that men are the ones who feel they aren't getting enough sex. All those poor bottled-up businessmen come home to that time-honored excuse, "Not-Tonight-Dear-I-Have-A-Terrible-Headache!" But the reality is that a surprisingly high proportion of women feel equally (if not *more*) sexually dissatisfied, even though many of them try to suppress their dissatisfaction because they feel that their sexual urges are abnormal.

"My mother never talked about sex to me," explained Lindy, a thirty-three-year-old dental assistant from Trenton, New Jersey. "All she said was, it's a duty that every wife has to perform for her husband, without complaining. I sometimes feel sad that she must have conceived me out of duty, rather than fun.

"It took me ten years, two husbands and five years of analysis to learn that my own sexual feelings weren't obsessive or weird or perverted. I wanted sex every single day. I thought about sex all the time. I mean—not necessarily intercourse but all the things that go with sex, like teasing and flirting and romance.

"I guess I was like a volcano that was told that it was wrong to erupt. But once I finally understood that it *wasn't* wrong—that erupting was what volcanoes were naturally meant to do—then, boy, I erupted, and I've never had so much pleasure in my whole life."

Anne-Marie, thirty-one, a drugstore manager from Chicago, Illinois, told me, "My mom was wonderful about the facts of life. She was caring and broad-minded, and she told me everything there was to know. I guess what she hadn't taken into account was that my first live-in lover was going to be the kind of man who needed sex only once a week—every Sunday morning before breakfast—and who shied away from anything remotely different, like sharing a shower, or making love in front of the fire. And he wouldn't let me walk around the apartment nude! I loved him, that's why I stayed with him. At least, I thought I loved him. But he never gave me an orgasm once, and after two years he began to make me feel that I was some kind of dirty-minded nymphomaniac, and that my family was like Sandstone or something." (Sandstone was a free-sex community in California in the 1970s.)

Then there was Jennifer, a twenty-two-year-old airline hostess from Seattle, Washington. "I was always interested in boys and sex, ever since I was about twelve. I used to read all the dirty bits in Judith Krantz novels, chauffeurs making love to their mistresses, stuff like that, and I used to have fantasies about meeting strange men at parties or at bus stations and making love to them in hotel rooms. My favorite fantasy was that I owned a stable, and that there was a really handsome, sulky stable-boy who used to trap me in the hayloft and lift up my dress and make love to me. I used to lie back on my bed and slowly lift up my dress and imagine that it was the stable-boy who was doing it. I made up a name for him, David; and sometimes when my parents were out I used to talk to him out loud. You know, things like, 'Oh, David, you mustn't kiss me! Oh, David, don't touch my knee! Oh, David, you mustn't touch my breasts like that!' I used to slide my hand into my bra and squeeze my nipples and pretend that it was David. Then I used to tug my panties up tight between my legs and tell him I didn't want him to make love to me; but all the time I kept tugging my panties again and again so that I was giving myself this really exciting feeling. My panties used to get really wet and slippery, and I used to tug them and tug them until they were tucked right up into my cunt. Then I used to run my fingers very gently and delicately all around my cunt, feeling how swollen my cunt-lips were, feeling how wet my pubic hair was, feeling how deep my panties had tucked themselves in. In my mind it was David touching me, David exploring me. He was strong and he was rough, but when it came to touching me, he was always real gentle. He hooked his fingertip around my panties and eased them out of me, and rolled them down my thighs. Then he touched me some more . . . real slowly, which was just me tantalizing myself. At the same time he kept on caressing my breasts and gently stroking my nipples. I've always loved having my breasts caressed when I'm making love . . . you'd be amazed how many men forget to touch your breasts once they've taken your panties off. At first I used to massage my nipples with body-lotion, but then I tried massaging them with juice from my cunt instead, and for a while that was a terrific turn-on because I imagined it was David doing it—touching my cunt and then rolling my nipples between his wet slippery fingers.

"I never used anything for masturbation except my fingers. I developed a way of sliding my left thumb into my cunt, and tugging gently downwards, while my index finger massaged my bottom. Then I used to flick my right middle finger very quickly and lightly over my clitoris. I didn't know it was called a clitoris when I first started doing it. I was only about thirteen. But I guess I learned a whole lot about myself sexually by touching myself. I used to meet girls who said they would never *dream* of touching themselves, let alone masturbating; but I guess that what they said and what they did in private were two different things.

I still masturbate quite often, for no other reason except that I like it and I need the sexual release, particularly when I'm traveling long-distance and have to stay overnight in a hotel. I don't fantasize about David the stable-boy any longer—no! But I do have a recurring fantasy about a strange man taking me out for the evening, and I'm not wearing anything at all except high heels and a pearl choker and a fur coat. I sit in these ritzy restaurants and let the coat slide down off my shoulders, not showing anything, but making it clear to everybody who's watching me that underneath the coat, I'm naked.

"When I was a teenager, I genuinely believed that I was a nymphomaniac. That didn't stop me from masturbating. I felt too much of a sexual urge to be able to stop. But then we moved to a better neighborhood and I met a whole group of six or seven girls who were just as interested in boys and sex as I was. We used to meet regularly at each other's houses and discuss what it was actually going to be like when we made love, and what a man's penis actually felt like. All of us used to ache to be married, so that we could have sex. That shows you how innocent we were—we thought you had to be married!

"We used to steal these sex magazines from one girl's brother, who kept dozens of them in his closet, thinking that nobody knew about them. We used to read all the stories out loud—stuff like, 'He thrust his huge member between her parted lips, and she sucked him as fiercely as if she hadn't eaten or drunk for a week.' We started off by slipping our hands into our panties when we read these stories, but after a while we weren't so shy with each other, and we used to undress and masturbate quite openly.

"I remember one summer afternoon there was six of us there and I was lying back on the bed while Kate was reading this sexy story called 'Midnight Lusts' that was supposed to be a classic. It was about two girls who make love to this one man called Ted, and they wind up sucking him together, one of them sucking his balls while the other sucks his cock.

"It was an incredibly erotic story, and while Kate was reading it we were all getting really turned on. Anna was rubbing herself and pressing her thighs together and moaning out loud. I had my legs wide apart and my eyes closed, and I was flicking my clitoris really quickly. I could picture these two girls licking and sucking and rubbing Ted's cock just as vividly as if I was there. The story described how his glans grew larger and larger inside this girl's mouth, and she could taste it and smell it.

"While Kate was reading, I suddenly felt somebody else touching my cunt, strange fingers. I opened my eyes in surprise and saw it was Sheila . . . she was a redheaded girl who used to live across the street. She was very pretty, with that really wavy reddish-blonde hair, and white skin, and enormous white breasts with tiny pink nipples which I always used to envy. Even her pubic hair was reddish-blonde—reddish-blonde pubic hair with very bright pink cunt lips. They almost clashed!

"I didn't know what to do at first, but Sheila smiled at me and pressed one finger to her lips and kept stroking and massaging my cunt. The feeling was so good that I closed my eyes again and pretended it was just a fantasy.

"Sheila touched me everywhere, in that incredibly gentle way that only a woman can do. She massaged my clitoris, and rolled my cunt-lips between her fingers, and slipped her fingers up inside me. She touched my bottom with one slippery fingertip, running it around and around until it tingled. Then she slid her finger right up inside, and that was the first time I discovered *that* particular kind of pleasure.

"Kate was reading how Ted's cock bulged and suddenly filled up the girl's mouth with sperm. The other girl kissed her, open-mouthed, and licked all round her mouth so that she could have his sperm instead.

"At that moment I had a climax that made the whole bed shake; and so did two of the other girls. I literally saw stars.

"In time, all of us girls went our different ways. Some of us got married; I went off to join the airline. But there's one thing that group experience taught me, and that was that almost all women are intensely curious and interested in sex . . . that if they're educated properly and they have no inhibitions about lovemaking, then there's a whole lifetime of pleasure just waiting for them.

"As far as I see it, a lot of their problems lie

with the fact that not many women realize that it's quite normal to feel strong sexual urges. They think they're alone, the way I used to. They think it's somehow wrong, or shameful, do you know what I mean? And the trouble is that men kind of reinforce that point of view because very few men know anything about a woman's urges or even her anatomy. My first lover had no idea that a woman pees from a different hole than the one she uses for making love. Can you believe that? A twenty-eight-year-old man, totally ignorant about sex. And he couldn't believe how often I wanted sex. 'You're sex-mad,' he used to say. But the fact is I wasn't, and I'm not. I simply refuse to pretend that I'm not feeling sexy when I do feel sexy.

"Sex doesn't dominate my life. I don't think about it all the time; just like I don't think about food all the time. But when I'm hungry, I'm not ashamed to sit down and have something to eat."

One reason why many women feel sexually frustrated is that their domestic situation doesn't allow them to express their character in any other way except for taking care of their home, their children and their husband.

He goes to work and releases much of his energy and his tensions on being aggressive and authoritative and creative, while *she* remains at home where a large percentage of her talent and her imaginative powers are never stretched—never even called upon, sometimes.

He receives daily appreciation and acclaim from his peers, and in many work situations, a certain amount of complimentary attention from other women. *She* has to rely almost entirely on the strength of his affection for her in order to evaluate her worth. As one homemaker from Pittsburgh put it to me, "Apart from my husband, the only man I see all day is Phil Donahue."

Because of this, a high percentage of women have a strong and frequent need for lovemaking. Not necessarily full intercourse, but kissing and caressing and any kind of demonstration that the men in their lives still find them exciting.

Of course a man who's been working all day finds it just as difficult to be sexually appreciative as a woman who's been running a home. But the "Not-Tonight-Dear-I've-Had-A-Hard-Day-At-The-Office" factor can have just as destructive an effect on a sexual relationship as the "Headache" factor.

One of the greatest problems is that many women find it extremely difficult to tell their partners about the urgency of their sexual appetites. Either they feel embarrassment or shame because they want to make love so frequently; or else they have the kind of partner who doesn't usually like discussing sex; or else they themselves find it almost impossible to put their sexual needs into words.

After all, very few women are brought up with a balanced, factual, unembarrassed sexual vocabulary. One of the first tasks I am faced with whenever I talk to a woman about her sexual feelings is to establish sexual words that she can feel happy about using in the context of normal conversation. Some women are quite happy to call their vaginas a "cunt" or a "pussy". Others prefer more gynecological terms. Still more have their own pet-names or nick-names for their sexual parts. I interviewed one young woman in San Francisco who insisted on calling her vagina "Mrs. Slotbox."

There is plenty of sexual discussion of a generalized kind in women's magazines and on TV talk shows. But we live in a society in which few families have open sexual conversations, and in which very few people are equipped with the vocabulary and the self-knowledge to have a constructive conversation about their sexual desires.

How would you explain to the man in your life that you usually feel like sex six or seven times a week? Could you even *consider* raising the subject? There are many women who can't.

Lois, a 21-year-old fabric designer from Chicago, Illinois, told me, "I was very disappointed when I started sharing my life with Wayne. Before he moved in, we were making love twice a day every day. I didn't expect it to carry on forever at that degree of intensity, you know. But I did expect more than I got. I found myself getting migraines and long periods of depression. I found that I was always arguing with people—not necessarily Wayne, but with everybody and anybody—the checkout girl at the market, my friends at work, even my mother. I expected regular sex. I expected *lots* of sex. But after the first couple of weeks, Wayne seemed to be more interested in walking in through the door, flopping himself down on the couch, opening a six-pack and glueing his eyes to the World Series.

"I began to think that he only loved me for my icebox and my television and for the sandwiches I brought him while he watched the sport.

"I tried to talk to him about it, but Wayne is one of those guys who gets easily embarrassed when you start talking about personal things like sex. In fact he got really angry, as if I was trying to criticize his manhood or something. He kept shouting, 'What's the problem? Don't I satisfy you or something?' He didn't want to hear the truth—he *could* satisfy me, he *did* satisfy me, but he wasn't satisfying me often enough.

"One of the worst feelings was that I'd made a terrible mistake . . . that *I* was somehow to blame.

Maybe I wanted too much sex, maybe there was something wrong with me. Maybe I wasn't doing enough to make Wayne feel excited. The terrible thing was that I loved him, I really loved him, but he was absolutely incapable of talking about sex. Once I'd asked him how much he wanted my cunt, just in play, you know. But he went crazy. He said he didn't like to hear a woman talking dirty, especially *his* woman.

"What made the situation worse was that even though he made love to me so seldom, he was always incredibly jealous and possessive. I'd only have to wear a short skirt or a lowcut blouse and he would go totally ape."

When she wrote to me, Lois was feeling, understandably, that her relationship with Wayne was pretty much over. Although she still loved him, the physical and mental effects of sexual frustration had made her feel irritable, depressed, and worst of all, it had lowered her opinion of herself as an attractive and sexually-arousing young woman.

I come across this kind of sexual problem time and time again. Mostly, you can trace it back to the man's immaturity and sexual ignorance—neither of which is usually the man's own fault. Often, he'll have a history of puritanically-minded parents, a broken home, or an awkward and unsatisfactory initiation into sex which has affected his attitude toward making love. Regardless of those old smoking-room tales about genial fathers initiating their sons by taking them to visit Madam Kitty's bordello, my research has shown that at least seventy percent of men who first had sex with a prostitute suffered long-term sexual problems. Most of those problems were rooted in the fact that they were subsequently unable to understand that most women expect intercourse to be very much more than the mechanical release of a simple physical tension. They expect it to be an expression of affection, of excitement, of ongoing love.

What's more, an extraordinary seventy-three percent of the men I talked to thought that lovemaking should occur when *they* felt like making love; and admitted that the idea of the woman in their lives needing sex more frequently "hadn't occurred to them."

Charles, a thirty-one-year-old airline mechanic from Philadelphia, said, "There's no way that you can suggest to me that my wife is sexually frustrated, never."

And this was a man whose wife had written to me because Charles was making love to her fewer than three times a month.

As Jeannie, a twenty-seven-year-old research assistant from Phoenix, Arizona, told me, "If more men realized how much lovemaking their wives really wanted, they'd have the time of their lives."

So don't believe for a moment that the man in your life knows everything there is to know about sex, no matter how many men's magazines he might have read. The "Playboy Advisor" may have told him all about multiple orgasms and clitoral stimulation and the calorific value of sperm. But unless he's been given a reasonable education in the sexual functions of his own body and in the sexual functions of a woman's body—as well as a comprehensive course in lovemaking and sexual fulfillment— it's very unlikely that he'll be equipped to deal with all the day-to-day difficulties that can arise in a full-time long-term sexual relationship.

It's also very unlikely that he'll understand the full extent of your day-to-day demands.

There's no use in complaining about it. No sexual difficulty was ever solved by complaining. If you feel that you need more lovemaking—not just intercourse or oral sex but all the affection and pleasure of being close, and if it makes you feel depressed or lonesome or frustrated—then it's up to you to change your sex life yourself.

It's in your power to give yourself the sex life you always dreamed of.

As I said earlier, the less sexually-motivated partner often has to make the most effort in bed in order to revive a sexual relationship. But if the less sexually-motivated partner doesn't even realize what's wrong or how to deal with the problem, then the more sexually-motivated partner is going to have to nudge him a little. Or *her*, as the case may be.

Sheila, a thirty-eight-year-old preacher's wife from Denver, Colorado, said, "Early in our married life, I used to reach orgasm fairly regularly. But as the years went by, I began to find it more and more difficult. I needed Frank to do other things to me apart from ordinary intercourse. I wanted him to touch me with his fingers or with his tongue, perhaps. But I simply couldn't find the words to tell him what I wanted him to do, and we didn't have the kind of relationship where I could have shown him. He would have thought I was acting like a harlot. He thought I was complaining that he was making love to me too often, and he started to leave me alone for days on end."

My advice to Sheila was to forget about trying to explain her frustration and to *show* her husband how she felt. One sexual action is often worth a thousand words.

In Sheila's case, it wasn't particularly easy. Her husband was a man of God, and was very reticent about sex. He preached modesty and temperance to his congregation, and tried to set an example in his own private life. In other words, it would have been highly inappropriate for Sheila to have danced into the bedroom in a Frederick's-of-Hollywood tasseled bra and open-crotch G-string.

But she did find a way. Let her describe it herself.

"Every time we made love, I kissed him and told him how much I loved him. I made it real plain to him that he had pleased me and that I had enjoyed myself. But then I lay back with my nightdress still lifted, closed my eyes, and slowly rubbed myself with my fingers, just the way I like it, rubbing my clitoris around and around with one hand and gently tugging at my sex lips with the other.

"The first time I did it, it took some nerve, I'll admit. Frank took hold of me and said, 'What are you doing?' He was pretty upset. 'Aren't you satisfied?' he asked me.

"I said, 'Of course I'm satisfied. But I need to have a climax, too.'

"He said, 'Well, I could have done that, if only I'd known. You never told me though, did you?'

"I said, 'No, I didn't, and I'm sorry. I should have. But now you know, why don't you try?'

"So I took his hand and showed him how to touch my sex so that he could give me a climax. I kept having to tell him to go more gently, but after a while he was doing it beautifully. I lay back on the pillow again and closed my eyes, and Frank kept rubbing my sex. He kissed my mouth and he kissed my breasts, and when he saw that I was getting all flushed and excited and that my nipples were rising up, he started to get excited again, too. I opened my eyes and I could see his cock sticking right up, all red and hard and still shiny from making love. I held his cock in my hand and gently stroked him up and down, too . . . not because I felt that I had to give him another climax, but because holding his hard cock in my hand turned me on and made it easier for me to reach my own climax. Well, you *did* tell me to be selfish about reaching my own climax.

"When it came, my climax washed over me like a wonderful warm wave. It was so beautiful. I felt a warm wet spattering on my breasts, and when I opened my eyes I saw that Frank had climaxed, too.

"It took him a while to understand that I almost *always* wanted a climax when we made love; and that wanting a climax didn't mean for a moment that he wasn't arousing me. Exactly the opposite. He *was* arousing me. He *was* turning me on, and I couldn't bear to lie there after our lovemaking was over feeling like I'd hiked nine-tenths of the way up the mountain only to be told that I couldn't get to the top."

A great many husbands and lovers display their sexual ignorance by failing to understand that women *do* need climaxes . . . but that most women find it extremely difficult to attain a climax during normal intercourse. In the immortal words of Meg Ryan in the movie *When Harry Met Sally*: "Most women, at one time or another, have faked it."

Like many men, Billy Crystal replies, "Not with me they haven't." But *you* know as well as I do that most women fake climaxes, some of them quite regularly. They fake climaxes for several reasons. Either they didn't really feel like making love and want to get it over with as quickly as possible; or their lover is making love to them uncomfortably or painfully and they want to finish quickly without hurting his feelings; or they don't believe that they are capable of reaching a climax, and are simply trying to stage a grand finale in a manner which they think will give their lover a sense of pleasure and pride.

I have had scores of letters from women who have been married for years and years, and have never experienced a "real" climax (although they dare not tell their partners).

One of the key secrets to having frequent and satisfying sex is to make sure that you *do* have regular climaxes . . . *real* climaxes, and that your lover is not only aware that you need them but knows how to give them to you, too.

If you know for sure that you can attain a satisfying climax, and your lover knows for sure that he can give it to you, both of you will have a compelling incentive to make love far more often and far more enthusiastically.

Frequent sex to most women is an affirmation not only of their sexual attractiveness but of their partners' interest in them as a whole personality. One of the most striking differences between the sexual response of men and women is that men can be strongly and immediately aroused by pictures of people they have never met and are never likely to meet. They can be turned on by photographs of breasts and vaginas which don't even show their owners' faces. Time and time again, I find men's sex magazines in which a whole page is taken up by nothing except a pin-sharp, full-color picture of a wide-open vulva . . . no face visible, no introduction necessary. Men's immediate sexual response is visual (although that doesn't mean for a moment that they don't need love and reassurance, too).

Women on the other hand require a personality with their penises. As author Gay Talese pointed out in his sex-epic *Thy Neighbor's Wife*, "Few women could be aroused by the sight of an erect penis *unless* they were warmly disposed to the man who was attached to it." A marriage therapist had told him, "If a man is a stranger to a woman, his penis is foreign to her, and she is not likely to want it inside of her, because then her person would be invaded. But if it is not alien to her, if it is part of somebody she knows, trusts, desires a relationship with, then she can take it into her, embrace it, and feel in harmony with it."

For that reason, women hardly ever respond to pictures of nude men in magazines, and my own research has shown that only a very few women ever use pictures of unknown nude men as a stimulus to lone masturbation. (Having said that, many women enjoy looking with their partners through magazines depicting sexual acts . . . particularly as a stimulus to lovemaking.)

Because lovemaking is a physical realization of their entire relationship with their partner, the consequences for women of not having enough sex can frequently be deep and disturbing. Much of the time, you won't consciously be aware that your problem is sexual. Men make coarse remarks about depressed or argumentative women, "Oh—what *she* needs is a good fuck." But it's surprising how often there's a grain of truth in that coarseness.

Having frequent sex does very much more than release tensions. It raises your self-esteem; it re-establishes your closeness with your partner; it defines your status as a woman; it demonstrates that somebody needs you and desires you . . . not just every now and then, for the sake of releasing his own bottled-up semen, but all the time.

Here's Andrea, twenty-eight, a hotel cleaner from Scottsdale, Arizona. Andrea is blonde and petite (5'2"), with slim legs and a very large bosom. "My husband Bob started to work the nightshift. Because of that, we got to see less and less of each other. When I was awake, he was sleeping, and when I was in bed, he was gone. It got so as we weren't making love more than two or three times a month.

"I started to get depressions and headaches and I started feeling really worthless and unattractive. Before Bob went on the nightshift, I always used to dress up and have my hair fixed regularly. I used to groom myself, if you know what I mean. Wax my legs, paint my nails, wear sexy underwear, things like that. But when we stopped having sex so often, I lost interest in myself. I just didn't bother anymore.

"If it hadn't been for Roy, I wouldn't have figured out what was wrong with me. Roy was one of the bellhops. He had just turned twenty—I knew that because we'd held a birthday party for him. A tall young guy, a little slow, but very good-looking. Roy was always flirting with the girls and fooling around, and with me especially. He always used to call me 'Little Annie Fanny,' on account of my figure.

"Anyway, I was cleaning out the shower-stall in one of the rooms when Roy came in. He said the desk clerk wanted to know when the room was going to be ready because the guests had just called from the airport to say that they'd arrived early. Anyway, we just chatted away while I cleaned the tiles, and then Roy said something like, 'I always get the hots when I'm close to you . . . I just can't help it.'

"Well, I said, 'I'm an old married woman, you can't think things like that about me.'

"He said, 'Not so old, and what does it matter if you're married?'

"I said, 'Forget it, punk!' and pushed him. But do you know what he did? He turned on the shower and totally soaked me. I screamed. But then he got into the shower-stall with me and took me in his arms and kissed me—even though he was getting soaked, too.

"I guess there were all kinds of ways I could have reacted. I could have told him to cool down. I could have been angry. But the truth was, I felt flattered, and I felt turned on, too.

"I said, 'I'm all wet now. I'm going to have to change my overall.' He grinned at me and said, 'I'll help you.' He unbuttoned my cleaning overall, and of course I never wear anything underneath except for a bra and panties. They were white cotton, but they were all wet, so you could see right through them.

"I remember thinking to myself, 'I shouldn't be doing this.' But the urge to feel another man in my arms was stronger. Roy unfastened my bra, and squeezed my breasts in his hands. The shower was still spraying all over us, and he gently rubbed my nipples between his finger and thumb, and lifted them up so that the shower sprayed all over them. Then he sucked them, too, quite hard, taking the whole of the nipple right into his mouth, and how could I say no to him after that?

"He opened his shirt. His chest was very muscular and hard. I helped him unbuckle his belt, and tug down his soaking-wet 501s. He was very slim and muscular. He did body-building, you know? And he'd shaved off all of his pubic hair, so his cock was completely bare. It stuck out like a sculpture, really hard and clean and fantastic.

"I knelt down on the tiles and I took hold of his cock in both hands. It was enormous, completely hard. The head of it was like some sort of fruit, but with silky skin. I stuck out my tongue and I licked all the way around it, and then all the way down to his tight hairless balls. I'd never seen a grown man completely shaved before, and it excited me so much that I was breathless.

"I took his balls into my mouth one by one and licked them and sucked them and jiggled them up and down with my tongue. I don't know whether many women have ever sucked a man's balls like that, but it's incredible . . . a man's so strong and physical and yet his balls are so delicate. Then I licked right between his legs, and probed up his ass. He was hairless there, too, and water was pouring down between the cheeks of his bottom, tight muscular cheeks, and I curled up my tongue and pushed it up his ass as far as I could.

"Then I licked around his balls again, and back up to the head of his cock. He was tangling his hands in my hair and he was groaning, I swear it. I turned around in the shower so that I was kneeling with my back to him, and then I stretched back my head and took his cock into my mouth. I took a deep breath and let him slide his cock right into my throat. I could feel the head of his cock so far down my throat that I thought I was going to choke, and his wet bare balls were pressed against my nose.

"For some reason, I felt that I wanted him to *take* me, to invade every single part of me where nobody had gone before. I sound like *Star Trek*, don't I? But I felt like I needed to be *used* a little; not raped, but treated like a woman; treated like a sex object.

"I turned around and sucked his cock harder and harder, deeper and deeper. I just loved the feel of his cock pressing against the roof of my mouth. I took hold of his balls in my hand and gently squeezed them, and I could feel them wrinkle and tighten up. He didn't say anything. He was so tensed up. Then suddenly I felt him quiver, and I knew what was happening. I took his cock out of my mouth and held it about two or three inches in front of my face, and I gave it two or three quick rubs.

"He didn't make a sound. But thick white sperm suddenly came shooting out of his cock, hot like milk, and I let it drop all over my face, all over my eyelashes and my cheeks and my lips, and then I took his cock into my mouth, and I sucked out the last drops of sperm that he couldn't shoot out by himself.

"I wiped my face with my hand, and my hand was filled with sperm. I licked it and swallowed it, and it tasted more delicious than anything that I'd ever tasted before; because it tasted like a man who wanted me. It tasted like a man who thought I was feminine and sexy.

"I never let Roy make love to me. I mean, I never let him enter my cunt. You'll probably think that it's totally ridiculous, totally hypocritical, but if I had ever let him make love to me, I would've felt I was being unfaithful. Whereas what we did, now and again, a few kissing and sucking sessions in empty rooms, that was just fun. No—correction—that was just reassurance. Roy never asked anything more; and I was never inclined to give him anything more.

"Occasionally, I'd say to him, 'I feel like a drink,' and that was a code between us; because we'd slip into one of the empty rooms and I'd quickly open his pants and take out his cock. Then I'd suck him and rub him until he climaxed. I know that some women would think that I was being unfaithful to Bob by sucking another man's cock, but I didn't see it that way. It was exciting, it made me feel feminine and sexy all over again, and the worst that could happen was that my love life with Bob could get some of the spice back into it. It was kind of like having an affair but not having an affair. Maybe I used Roy more than I should have done. But I started taking more interest in myself and the way I dressed, because at first I was dressing for Roy. I started polishing my nails and waxing my legs and smartening myself up.

"What happened was that I grew more confident about myself sexually. I grew more confident about my ability to attract Bob. These days we're still working nights and days, and scarcely see each other, but when we *do* see each other, for those few hours each day, and each weekend, we're really hot. The other day I came home from work and Bob was fast asleep in bed. I took off my clothes and climbed into bed with him. I could still taste Roy in my mouth, that delicious dry salty taste. I started to suck Bob's cock even before he was awake. He was quite soft at first, and I could get all of his cock into my mouth, right up to his balls.

"It was amazing. As he gradually woke up, his cock grew bigger and harder, and it seemed to stretch my mouth so much that I could hardly take it all in. He ran his fingers through my hair and caressed my back and my shoulders. Then he lifted me up on top of him and kissed me, and then he pushed his cock right up into my cunt as far as it would go. I could feel it because it was still wet and cold and slippery with my own saliva.

"We had one of the fiercest fucks that we'd ever had—ever—so fierce that I climaxed twice, which I'd never ever done before.

"Our married life is still difficult. We still don't see each other often enough. We still don't make love often enough. But then, who does? All I know is that I'm still attractive to men; and having that confidence has made all the difference in the world."

2

The Ins
And Outs Of Love

Even today, with so much "how-to" information about sex so readily available in books and magazines, many lovers don't know nearly as much about their erotic responses as they ought to.

It's a fallacy to think that we live in a sexually liberated age in which every intelligent adult knows everything there is to know about making love. We are still the victims of prudishness, of rumor, of misinformation . . . and most of all we are still the victims of our own overwhelming shyness.

I still receive reports from doctors about newly-wed couples who simply don't know how to make love properly. One young Cleveland bride was desperate because she couldn't get pregnant, no matter how much semen she swallowed.

And judging from the questions that even experienced lovers ask, I don't have any hesitation in suggesting that a *majority* of couples are missing out on much of the pleasure and satisfaction that sex could be giving them, for no other reason except they don't really know what to do or how to do it.

"They taught us about human reproduction at high school," said Donna, twenty-three, a real-estate salesperson from Darien, Connecticut. "They showed us diagrams and models of all the sexual parts, male and female, and how they worked. They told us all about having babies. They even managed to tell us about the various methods of contraception. But when I first made love to a man, I didn't understand anything. I simply didn't know what to do. Did he expect me to lie there while he made all the moves? How was I supposed to act? Was I supposed to moan and groan and look all vampish? Would he like it if I touched his penis? Supposing he didn't like it? Was I supposed to kiss his penis? I'd heard about fellatio, but I wasn't sure that I could ever do it. And as for allowing a man to kiss *me* between my legs . . . how could he even want to? And how could I let him? I used to get so wet, he'd find it disgusting.

"It took me three very bad affairs and a whole lot of heartache before I found a man who knew anything about sex and who treated me wisely and sympathetically. Before that, I'd had one of the clumsiest sexual relationships you could ever imagine, followed by another that was closer to rape than sex—as well as some bad beatings and some glorious black eyes. Then I had an affair with an older man who was kind and gentle but who didn't pay any attention to *my* sexual needs. Once he was finished, that was it. It was time to turn over and go to sleep.

"I don't know who to blame for my sexual experiences, but what happened to me wasn't unusual or peculiar. I've talked to my friends, and I'd guess that thousands of girls—I don't know, maybe millions of girls—suffer the same agonies that I suffered. They go out into the world brimming with sexuality, brimming with love, but as innocent and ignorant as spring lambs. They think they're going to meet men who know all about sex . . . some kind of Charles Boyer character who's going to teach them what it's all about. Somebody who's going to give them wonderful orgasms and all those ocean waves and fireworks you read about in romantic novels.

"It's not like that at all. Most of the men you meet know nothing about women. Sometimes they don't even know how to put their cocks in properly. They don't know how to touch you, they don't know how to kiss you. Especially the really straight guys, the guys who've never seen a porno movie. At least the guys who've seen a porno movie have *some* idea what to do, even if they expect you to wear stockings and a garter-belt and go 'ohh, ohh,' all the time and keep changing positions, and they always want to spray their come all over your bottom."

As she correctly guessed, Donna's experiences with sex were not unusual. Considering that making love is one of mankind's most important preoccupations, the ignorance and hostility surrounding it are quite incredible. There is more accurate and helpful information put out about golf than there is about sex . . . and I'm speaking with the experience of a quarter of a century in the business of sexual counseling and sexual guidance.

I would like to assume that by picking up this book, you're a mature person who's interested in the pleasures and joys of sex, and that you're looking for more frequent sex—six-times-a-week sex—and more exciting sex.

I would also like to assume that you do know something about basic sexual anatomy and how the male and female sexual organs respond to erotic stimulation. If you're not sure (and, believe me, there's no shame in that, because millions of people aren't completely sure) then I'd recommend some of my other books like *How To Drive Your Man Wild In Bed*, *How To Drive Your Woman Wild In Bed*, and *How To Be The Perfect Lover*.

In those books you'll discover detailed descriptions of your sexual anatomy, as well as step-by-step explanations of how your body responds when you make love.

If you want to improve the frequency and the quality of your lovemaking, however, you and your lover must share in a long and detailed session of physical exploration—an open and intimate journey of mutual discovery.

Mutual Discovery Sessions have been one of the most successful aids yet to rescuing jaded sexual relationships. Occasionally, a couple have been on the verge of divorce because of their sexual problems, but have found that a Mutual Discovery Session has brought them back together again with such affection and such sexual intensity that they feel "it's just like the first night we slept together . . . only better."

Familiarity doesn't necessarily breed contempt, but after a few years, any intense relationship can become fractured and dull and difficult. The first thrill wears off, and then, if you're not a knowledgeable and practised lover, it's almost impossible to keep up the level of erotic excitement.

Your sexual interest begins to wane—not because you don't love each other any more. In fact, after several years together, you probably love each other more than ever. But where's the freshness? Where's the creativity? Where's the jangle of nerves when he kisses your breasts and his penis slides inside you?

I talked to dozens of couples about reviving their sex lives, and again and again I came across the same complaint. "He used to turn me on, but he never did it particularly well, and now that we've been together for so long . . ." "We make love, but she never touches my cock, never . . . except to push it back in again if it slips out of her. She never rubs it and she certainly never gives me a blowjob." "He hasn't given me a climax in four years. He makes love like he's eating a sandwich. Gobble, gobble, gobble, that's it, finished. Sometimes he remembers and tries to masturbate me so that I can have a climax, too, but he's always so rough and so hurried, so I pretend. He thinks he's a great lover." "She's had some hormone imbalance, and her periods have been getting worse. Sometimes we can't make love for three weeks out of the month. It's driving me crazy, but I don't know what to do. I think it's driving her crazy, too, but how can you have intercourse with a woman who's bleeding all the time?"

My mailbag is full of problems like these. They're worrying, they're irksome, and when you're feeling sexually frustrated, the smallest chip of shingle in your shoe can feel like Mount Baldy.

The trouble is, sexual problems are always more difficult to solve than any other kind of personal problems because they're so intimate—and because they're all tangled up with embarrassment and pride. Every man likes to believe that he's the best lover in the world, and few women have the nerve to tell them that they're not. Similarly, just as few men have the nerve to tell the women in their lives that their lovemaking is awkward and unresponsive.

If you have tax problems, you don't feel ashamed to go to your accountant and ask for his advice. If you're feeling under the weather, you don't have any qualms about calling your doctor. You don't blush when you take your car to the garage for servicing. So why should you feel too embarrassed to seek assistance when your sex life starts to run down?

Well, the fact is that—for better or worse—you

usually do. Sex for most of us is still a highly ticklish topic—particularly our own sexual performance. Unless social attitudes change dramatically (and there's no indication that they will), sex is going to stay a sensitive and highly personal topic for many decades to come.

In some ways, I approve of that. While I'm the firmest believer in open sexual discussion and the widest possible dissemination of sexual information, I don't believe that the so-called "open marriage" of the 1960s was particularly beneficial to the couples who took part in it, nor helpful to ordinary couples who were trying to make the very most of their own love lives. Most of the "free sex" era was sexual exhibitionism dressed up as quack sociology.

Your sex life is your own. You can have the most exciting and ecstatic of sexual experiences *within your existing relationship*. You may have convinced yourself that the man or woman in your life isn't particularly interested in you any more, and that you have nothing to look forward to for the rest of your life but dull, infrequent, and routine sexual intercourse . . . but you're wrong.

Your sexual revival is within your grasp. Starting tonight, you and your partner can become one of those glowing, closely-knit couples who have sex every night of the week, every day of the week, and sometimes more often. You can liberate all of your inhibitions, you can release all of your sexual desires.

You can have sex whenever and however you feel like it. You have the desire. You have the potential. And when you learn how to do it, you will instantly feel the benefits.

All of the sexual consultants to whom I talked during my research for this book agreed that:

* Frequent sex is good for your self-confidence.

* Frequent sex is good for your physical fitness and general well-being.

* Frequent sex gives you a more positive and creative attitude toward life, and will have a direct beneficial effect on anything that you're trying to achieve, either at home or at work.

* Frequent sex makes you calmer, less irritable, and more capable of coping not only with your own daily problems but with the problems of other people.

* Frequent sex improves your self-image.

* Frequent sex helps you to explore the full potential of your emotions, your body, and your imagination.

* Without any exaggeration, frequent sex can change your life from top to bottom.

You may have sexual problems in your life; niggling little problems in your relationship with your partner. Some of those problems may not appear to be directly related to sex. Things like, who washes the dishes. Things like, what TV channel you're going to watch. Or maybe they're more serious difficulties, like your partner's failure to understand your ambitions or your intellectual needs.

But the fact remains that by enjoying frequent sex, by making up your mind that you and your partner are going to indulge yourselves in whatever erotic delights you can conjure up between you—not just on that second-honeymoon trip to Acapulco, not just on that special weekend when you heard about his promotion to senior manager, but every week, every night of the week—you will discover that most of the niggling little problems have mysteriously vanished, and that even the bigger problems, the problems that didn't appear to be sexually-related, are easier to deal with.

Here's Rosemarie, a thirty-two-year-old travel

agent from Portland, Oregon: "After my second daughter was old enough to go to nursery school, I went directly back to work in the travel business. I'd always been good at arranging flights and vacations. I've got one of those organizing minds. And I love the travel business.

"But my husband John seemed to resent the fact that I was concentrating all my attention on my job and ignoring him. One evening we had a few too many to drink, and all of his resentment came pouring out of him. He said he felt like a monk, being married to me. He said he didn't even know why he bothered to stay married. He felt bottled-up, frustrated. Whenever he wanted to have sex with me I was always too tired or too busy or not particularly interested. He said I stopped him dead right in the middle of foreplay once, while he was kissing my breasts, and said, 'My God, did I remember to book Mr. Greenbaum's flight to Delhi?'

"Well, I'm sorry to say that I *had* done that, for real. And although when I was drunk I accused John of being petty and picky and jealous of absolutely everything I did—a hypocritical pig who walked around on two legs, and all kinds of terrible things like that—he was right. He was absolutely right. The girls at work were wonderful; my job was wonderful; but our sex life had died a death.

"At first I tried to lay blame. You know—if our sex life was rotten, then it was all John's fault, because the sexual side of marriage was always my husband's responsibility. But the more I thought about it, the more I knew in my heart of hearts that I was kidding myself. I was so full of the girls, so full of my job . . . I was so fulfilled and satisfied that I'd almost forgotten about the sexual needs of the man I married. I'd almost forgotten about my own sexual needs, too. That can happen. You can put them out of your mind. But suddenly you can look at yourself and see what kind of a person you've turned into. Driven, yes. Ambitious, yes. Successful, loyal, a caring parent who reads stories to her kids and cooks terrific lasagne.

"But somehow all the roses and stars have gone out of everything. And the raunchiness, too, if you want to be truthful about it. The fucking and the kissing and the sweating and all of that."

Because so many couples like Rosemarie and John become sexually alienated from each other, I devised the Mutual Discovery Session. It can be used by any couple who want to improve their sexual relationship—whether they've just started living together or whether they've been married for more years than either of them can count.

The simple fundamental idea is that they spend two or three hours together discovering each other's bodies, discovering each other's desires, discovering each other's frustrations. It's amazingly liberating and therapeutic, but unlike convential therapy, it has immediate and very positive results . . . and results that last.

The aim of the Mutual Discovery Session is simply this: that, by the end of it, you and your partner should have agreed to make love *at least six times a week*—even if "making love" amounts to nothing more than a naked bedtime massage, or a prolonged bout of kissing (and, come on, fess up—when was the last time you kissed your partner the way you used to kiss when you first met each other?).

The Mutual Discovery Session is a time for both of you to talk about your love life with complete openness . . . to discuss your joys and your disappointments, your hopes and your fears, your fantasies and your fetishes. It is a time when both of you can say everything that you ever wanted to say to each other about sex but were afraid to.

A Mutual Discovery Session can only be arranged if you and your lover both agree to give it a try.

The basic agreement you have to reach with your lover is this: that it would do both of you good to discuss your sex life more openly. And even if you think that you're reasonably sexually satisfied already, it certainly wouldn't do you any harm to see what further pleasures you might be able to get out of the happy fact that you're both in love.

The truth is that almost everybody has some sexual fantasy or unfulfilled desire that they haven't told their lover about. And the truth is also that almost everybody has some nagging sexual dissatisfaction that they haven't told their lover about, either.

The Mutual Discovery Session is designed to bring both your fantasies and your irritations out into the open. At the same time, it will help both of you to let out of the closet any long-standing sexual inhibitions you might have been harboring.

Rosemarie and John tried a Mutual Discovery Session one afternoon, and in Rosemarie's words "it turned our sex-lives around. I found out things about John I'd never even guessed at. There were things he had always wanted me to do in bed, and he'd never been able to tell me. There were fantasies he'd had, incredible sexual fantasies, and I'd never even known. At the same time I found myself saying things to him that I'd always kept totally private. I thought it was going to be fun. I thought it was going to be sexy. But I didn't think it was going to be quite as shattering as it turned out to be. I look back on it now as the day when my whole sex life burst into flower."

So, what did Rosemarie actually do? And what

can *you* do, to turn your sex life around in a matter of hours?

First of all, as I said, you and your partner have to agree that it wouldn't hurt your sex life to discover or re-discover each other's sexual responses and fantasies. You don't need to expect any more out of it than that. So long as you both understand that the purpose of the session is not to attach blame for anything that might have been going wrong . . . not to accuse the man of dirty-mindedness or the woman of nymphomania . . . not to start arguing about impotence or frigidity or frustration or lack of caring.

You should set aside any difficulties that you might be having with your sex life. You're here to explore new possibilities, not to recriminate about past misunderstandings.

And the Mutual Discovery Session will give you the opportunity go right back to basics—right back to those days when your lover first touched you. It will give you the opportunity to learn and explore right from the very beginning . . . to correct mistakes and prejudices and to re-evaluate desires and dislikes.

To any lover who might be skeptical of trying it, may I say just this: out of thirty-five couples who agreed to take part in a test of Mutual Discovery Sessions, thirty declared themselves to be "gratified, pleased, and above all excited about the future." Every couple without exception reported a regular increase in the frequency of their lovemaking. Nineteen out of those thirty-five couples reported that for the first six months after their Mutual Discovery Sessions, they were still making love *on average* four times a week.

What a Mutual Discovery Session involves is that you and your lover should agree to spend at least three hours together, undisturbed by telephones, visitors or children, and to use that time to explore each other's bodies, each other's erotic responses, and to discuss without any restriction whatsoever your sexual urges and unfulfilled sexual needs.

The rules are simple, but *it is absolutely essential that you both stick to them.* There should be no expressions of shock, no declarations of distaste, no horrified cries of "You never told me you wanted me to do *that*!"

This is a time when you have both agreed to listen to each other, to learn and to explore. You discuss in detail almost every other aspect of your lives together—work, money, vacations, parents, children, food—why can't you do it in the most intimate and emotional area of all?

When you've picked your time, next pick your place. A bedroom is obviously ideal, but a comfortable living-room can be just as suitable. One Southern California couple had their Mutual Discovery Session in the open air, beside the pool.

Both of you should think about this session well in advance. Not only does thinking about it ahead of time increase the sense of erotic anticipation, but it gives both of you time to collect together any sexual material that may help you to show your lover just what turns you on the most. You could buy sexy videos that key on your particular sexual taste (such as *Deep Throat*); you could buy erotic books and magazines; or any number of sex toys, such as vibrators or ben-wa love-balls; or sexy clothing, like open-fronted panties or rubberwear or leather thongs or whatever turns you on.

The rule is: whatever your lover brings to this session, he or she must be able to do so freely, without criticism or disapproval. After all, the object is not for you to impose your sexual tastes on each other, but to discover each other's hidden sexual urges, and to bring out the very best in each other.

When the chosen time for your Mutual Discovery Session arrives, sit down together and make yourselves the following promise: that you are both seeking to discover each other, because of the affection you share, and that you are both looking for an even happier and more stimulating sex life. No looking back. Your new sex life starts here.

You can of course see the basic principle of the Mutual Discovery Session. It's the way in which every couple would ideally get to know each other sexually if society and social events would ever allow it. Instead of entering a sexual relationship haphazardly, couples would have a reasonable idea of each other's needs and each other's tastes, and have a sound training in sexual response. You don't often find out-and-out baseball fans having a particularly good time in the company of devoted watercolorists, so is it any surprise that a woman who gets deep fulfillment and satisfaction from oral sex should feel discontented in the company of a man who wouldn't lick a woman's vagina if you gave him a free Porsche and a weekend vacation in Florida?

Life and society, needless to say, are far from ideal and make sexual discovery prior to lovemaking not just awkward but almost impossible. A man is hardly likely to ask you, "Pardon me, but are you any good at cocksucking?" over cocktails-for-two; and there's no way that you can give a man a fifty-question test on sex while he's rowing you across the lake on a sunny afternoon. "Yes, I love the way you sing, but do you know what happens to my clitoris immediately prior to orgasm?"

So, social convention makes it pretty well impossible for you and your partner to discover in advance if you're sexually compatible or not. You can't reasonably arrange a Mutual Discovery Session on your first date. You probably wouldn't want to. But there's no reason in the world why you can't try it when you're several weeks or months or years into your relationship, and there's every reason in the world why you *should*.

To any lovers who express doubts, I always pose these two plain questions: "Do you remember what it felt like when you first made love to your partner? And would you like your lovemaking to feel that way again?"

Most lovers go into a Mutual Discovery Session expecting (with some anxiety) to find out that they haven't been satisfying their partner in bed. "I know he likes me to make the first move sometimes," confessed Rhoda, a twenty-four-year-old farmer's wife from Madison, Wisconsin. "And I know that I scarcely ever do it."

"After I've come, I don't usually bother to make sure that Jo-Beth's come, too," admitted twenty-nine-year-old Dick, a steelworker from Pittsburgh, Pennsylvania. "No matter how much I promise myself when I'm building up to it, I always lose interest after I've shot my load. All I feel like then is rolling over and catching some zees."

But in spite of what most lovers think they're going to discover, they're usually in for a fascinating and often pleasant surprise. If anything, they're going to find out that their lover frequently finds them much more sexually attractive than they ever realized. They're also going to find out that it was only their own reticence, their own inability to communicate to their lover how much sex they wanted, that led to a falling-off in the frequency of their lovemaking.

It's the old equation exemplified by the deteriorating relationship between Marty, a thirty-five-year-old airplane mechanic from Cleveland, Ohio, and his wife Marcia. "Right from the first night of our marriage, Marcia never seemed to show any wild interest in sex, and sometimes when I got into bed and put my arm around her, she used to snap, 'Get off, I don't feel like it.' In the end I stopped trying, except when I really needed it, because I was afraid of being rejected. All right, I guess you could say that I was afraid of looking like a fool. It was only when we tried one of these sessions that we both understood that we'd been acting like idiots all these years. We could have been fucking each other day in, day out. She liked making love as much as I did, but her momma had always said to her that it was disgusting for a woman to discuss sex with her husband. It would make him think she was cheap and easy. Anyway, we tried the Mutual Discovery Session and to tell you the truth, I wasn't expecting anything more than to find out why Marcia didn't like sex too often. What I actually found out was that I'd been married for five years to a girl who liked to have sex just as often as I did, if not more. It was a revelation. She kept asking me why I'd never fucked her in between her breasts. She's got huge breasts and she'd been dying for years to take my cock in between them and squeeze her breasts up and down with my cock trapped in between them until I had a climax and smothered them with sperm. Then she wanted me to massage the sperm into her breasts, to make them firmer, that's what she said. I couldn't believe what I was hearing. It was like somebody telling me that I'd just won the lottery. All of my fantasies come true. She wanted sex four or five times a week, that's what she told me. And most of all she wanted me to fuck her in between her breasts. All I can say is that Marcia's the queen of the universe now, as far as I'm concerned. She's always dragging me off to the bedroom. Quite often we don't even make it as far as the bedroom.

"You know what she did the other day? I was sitting on the couch watching the TV and Marcia came in and knelt between my legs. She kissed me, and called me her honey, and all the time she was kissing me she was opening my pants. Then she started rubbing my cock up and down with her hand, and kissing the end of it, and looking up at me with the dirtiest look on her face you could ever imagine.

"I could hardly believe what I was seeing and feeling. A month ago, before we did the Mutual Discovery thing, she never would have dreamed of doing anything like that. But she kept on rubbing, until I was groaning out loud. She was gripping my cock so tight that it was bulging, and she kept rubbing her thumb around and around on the hole, so that the head was all slippery with my juice, and her fingers were, too.

"Then she leaned forward, and unbuttoned her dress a couple of buttons, and lifted her right breast out of her bra. She gave me three quick rubs, and I shot sperm right up into the air. Some of it landed on her hair, but most of it shot over her breast. She squeezed her breast and pressed the nipple right up against my cock-hole, massaging my cock and her breast together until they were both all shiny and slippery. Then she put her breast back in her bra, and kissed me, and said, 'Now I've got you close to my heart.'

"If you had told me three weeks previous that my Marcia would ever do a thing like that, I would've said you were three clubs short of a set."

One of the most important points to remember

about your Mutual Discovery Session is that you must both be prepared to try *anything*. This, after all, is a time for you to set aside all of your inhibitions, all of your prejudices, all of your shyness. During the hours you spend in Mutual Discovery, the rule is that anything and everything goes. You must both agree that no matter what you do—no matter what you say—there will be no recriminations afterwards. In other words, no matter what secret desires or fantasies your partner admits to, don't hold it against him.

I'm not going to pretend for a moment that it will be easy for either of you to be so open. The whole reason you're going to try a Mutual Discovery Session is because you feel your love life has lost its forward momentum and needs some new energy. Like servicing an automobile, you can only give it that new energy with a complete strip-down and overhaul. That is what a Mutual Discovery Session is all about.

You've agreed with your partner to try out a Mutual Discovery Session. If your partner has expressed any reluctance, you've explained that it's a tried-and-tested way of improving your sex life. And even if he or she feels that you have nothing to gain, well, you surely have nothing to lose.

You've selected your time; you've selected your venue. You've bought all the books or magazines or videos that you think may arouse you. You've selected some sex aids, and maybe some erotic underwear. Now let's see how you and your partner can actually change your whole sex life in less than three hours.

3

How To Explore Your Lover's Body

"I hadn't deliberately dressed up to attract Doug sexually since we first dated," confessed twenty-four-year-old Davina, a bank teller from Omaha, Nebraska. "But when you suggested we get together in a Mutual Discovery Session, that gave me a special occasion to think about . . . a reason for dressing-up. Suddenly, after five years of marriage, it became important for me to make sure that I turned him on.

"I looked at myself and realized how much I'd let myself go. My hairstyle was okay and my dress was okay, but I wasn't really one hundred percent. I didn't *shine* the way I used to. And do you know? I thought, 'Doug deserves better than this. Just like *I* deserve better from him.'

"I had my hair highlighted and cut and styled. I manicured my nails. I plucked my eyebrows, waxed my legs and shaved off my pubic hair. I bought three new bras and three new pairs of panties as well as two G-strings. I bought a new blouse and two new sweaters and a new skirt.

"I bought some new perfume, too. Giorgio, from Beverly Hills, and Chanel. By the time Saturday afternoon arrived—which was the time when we'd planned to have our session together—I felt just as good as I did when I first met Doug at the county fair."

Davina was marvelous. A vivacious, energetic blonde with a firm belief in making the best of life. But she freely admitted that her sex life with Doug, a twenty-six-year-old realtor, had already become routine and "stale." They made love on average only three times a month, and she rarely reached orgasm. She felt that "something wasn't clicking . . . we both loved each other, we both enjoyed sex . . . but somehow we never managed to get together."

Davina's problem affects thousands of couples in long-term sexual relationships. After working all day, both partners feel like quiet and relaxation, rather than frantic sexual activity. The result is that they become increasingly non-communicative; and a couple who are non-communicative *out* of bed aren't going to be very successful when it comes to communicating *in* bed.

You know what they say about great oaks growing from little acorns. If you don't attend to it as soon as possible, the smallest neglect in a sexual relationship can eventually break your whole relationship apart . . . no matter how good every other aspect of it may be. There is nothing like sexual frustration to foster resentment. I receive scores of letters every month from men and women who have reached a point in their lives where they are nothing short of desperate simply because they feel unable to communicate their most intimate sexual desires to their partner.

Davina said, "I try to talk about sex with Doug, but he won't. He absolutely won't. I only have to mention sex and he gets angry. He makes me feel like a whore when all I want to do is make our marriage more exciting."

Davina was lucky to get Doug to agree to a Mutual Discovery Session. To be painfully honest, there are some men and women who just can't be persuaded to admit that anything is wrong with their sex lives, who just can't be persuaded to try Mutual Discovery or any other kind of sex therapy. This is particularly true of anybody who has suffered a sexually repressed upbringing or a distasteful or traumatic introduction to sex; and there are many more of those than there ought to be. Even today, we're a highly secretive society when it comes to matters of sex. We are to be condemned rather than congratulated that perfectly straightforward sex advisors like Doctor Ruth should be considered exceptional.

Michael, thirty-eight, a public relations consultant from Englewood, Colorado, said, "Sexual relations are private. As far as I'm concerned they're entirely a matter for husbands and wives to deal with on their own. I guess I learned about sex the same way that every man learns about sex. My father gave me the basic details when I was thirteen. The rest I learned from books, from lessons at school, and from my friends at college and in the Army. Sex is a pretty simple activity as far as I can make out. In fact, I'm amazed there are so many books about it. How much information do you need to put a pole into a hole? It's more difficult to put up a *tent* than it is to have sex; and yet how many books do you ever see on tents?"

Michael's wife Rhoda had written to me asking how she could explain to him that he never brought her to a climax, and that he made love to her "so seldom, and so quickly" that she was beginning to doubt that he loved her at all.

The plain truth of the matter was that as well-intentioned as he was, Michael knew very little about pleasing a woman sexually. His first sexual experience had occurred when he was fourteen with the daughter of his friend's Puerto Rican housemaid, and the experience had been "embarrassing, awkward and humiliating." It was hardly surprising that Michael's view of sex was nothing more than "a pole into a hole."

Let me make it quite clear, however, that you and your partner don't have to be suffering from any kind of sexual problem to benefit from a Mutual Discovery Session. You may both be very satisfied with your sex lives . . . but you could find out ways of making it even more exciting.

And, hand on your heart, are you yet making love six days a week, practically every week? You could be, and enjoying every single stimulating second of it.

You've chosen your time, your venue, and your partner has agreed that a Mutual Discovery Session is just what you need.

Make sure the room is warm and comfortable and completely private. Make sure there's no chance of you being interrupted, for any reason. Some fresh flowers, some soft cushions, some soothing background music . . . they all help to enhance the atmosphere. And how about a couple of bottles of champagne in the icebox as a way of relaxing and celebrating both at the same time? Be careful with the alcohol, though. It can have a depressant effect on your lover's erection, particularly if he's been having any trouble getting hard; and too much alcohol can occasionally release too many inhibitions. You don't want to end up fighting when you should be making love.

The very first thing to do is to take a shower or a bath together. This not only helps you both to relax, but gives you a reason for undressing that isn't entirely sexual. It slows down the pace and gives you both the opportunity to caress each other's naked bodies without immediately having intercourse. One of the most frequent complaints I receive from women is that their lovers "push it in, come, and then pull it out again," long before the women themselves are even aroused. If you share a shower before you even think about making love, you will both be well turned on by the time you're back in the bedroom (or living room, or wherever you've selected for your love-session).

It's important that you undress each other. During the early days of most sexual relationships, men take the trouble to unfasten bras, women take the trouble to unbuckle belts. But as a couple grow more familiar—as their sex life becomes routine—undressing each other is a pleasure they very often forget.

Here's Chet, thirty-two, a design-draftsman from Boston, Massachusetts: "I hadn't undressed Pam in *years*. When she'd filled up the tub, she called me into the bathroom and announced that she was ready. I don't know why, but I was dry-mouthed and my heart was pounding. My cock was already swelling in my pants. And this my *wife*, the woman I'd been married to for seven years! I couldn't believe that I felt so excited about her.

"She's very cute, very small, very blonde. She was wearing a cream-colored blouse, kind of floppy and soft with big sleeves, and a kind of cinnamon mini-skirt, and white ankle-socks. Her hair was fastened up with two big tortoiseshell barrettes. The first thing I did was hold her, and kiss her, and look into her eyes. She has these big wide sky-blue eyes, very innocent-looking.

"She said, 'You're supposed to undress me.' I said, 'I don't know where to start.' So she took out one of her barrettes, and said, 'You start at the top and work your way downward, I guess.'

"I took out the other barrette, and kissed her again. Then I cupped her breast through the silk of her blouse and squeezed it and caressed it. She has very small breasts, hardly any breasts at all, but I felt her nipple rise through the fabric, real hard and knobby and real distinct. I suddenly realized that I hadn't done that for as long as I could remember—cupped her breast through her clothes. I'd been married to her for so long that I guess I'd simply forgotten how to do it anymore.

"But it was such a turn-on. It was like I was making love to her for the very first time. My cock grew so hard that I thought I was going to bust out of my 501s.

"I unbuttoned her blouse, and opened it, and she was wearing a little white bra, it's so small that it's more like a training bra. But her nipples showed through it, bright pink, and they were sticking out stiff. She kissed me, and pushed her tongue right into my mouth, and caught hold of my hair, and I could tell that she was turned on, too.

"I took off her blouse and let it fall onto the bathroom chair. I could see her back in the mirror, narrow and pale; little shoulders like a bird, with that scraggly-curly blonde hair falling over them. I could hardly wait to make love to her. It was amazing. We'd both been working so hard that I guess we'd forgotten what it was like to make love to each other properly—not just a quick occasional fuck in the middle of the night.

"I tugged up her mini-skirt over her bottom. She may be small-breasted, but she has a gorgeous chubby round bottom. It looked in the mirror as if her bottom were bare at first—as if she wasn't wearing any panties. But when I reached my hand down between her thighs, I could feel that she was wearing a thong. Not one of the usual plain thongs she used for sunbathing, but a really tiny lacy one, with very thin elastic.

"The lips of her vagina were all wet and swelled up. In fact, she'd wet herself so much that her thong had gotten soaked and practically vanished into the slit of her vagina. I'd never known her so wet. I ran the tips of my fingers around and around her lips, gently massaging them. She always shaves herself, so she was totally slippery and smooth. Then I knelt down in front of her on the bathroom mat, and I eased the thong out from between her lips, and she stepped out of it.

"She said, 'Take it easy . . . we're supposed to undress each other first, take it slow.' But the sight of her vagina pouting at me like some young girl's mouth was more than I could resist. I kissed it, and gave it a single lick all the way from the back to the front, hesitating just for a second on the tip of her clitoris. Then I did what I was told and slowed up.

"I tugged down her skirt for her. Then I took each foot in turn, and unrolled her socks. She said, 'It's your turn now,' and so I stood up again.

"You wouldn't have thought that being undressed by your own wife could be so darned exciting. She unbuttoned my shirt, and then she reached inside it, right around to the back, and ran her nails all the way down my spine. I shivered. It was one of those feelings that really give you the shivers. Then she unfastened my cuffs and took my shirt right off me.

"I guess it was twice as exciting because she was naked, and I had to use all the self-control I could muster up not to put her down on the bathroom floor and make love to her there and then. But that wasn't the game, that wasn't in the rules. And, besides, I had the feeling that what we were doing was going to be a whole lot more enjoyable than that. In fact, I had the feeling that what we were doing was specifically designed to *stop* me from pushing her down onto the bathroom floor and making love to her without thinking about anything else.

"Once she'd taken off my shirt, she hunkered down on the bathroom floor in front of me and took off my socks, resting each of my feet on her shoulder in turn. She looked so natural and innocent, there was pale pink lipstick on her lips and pale pink lacquer on her fingernails and toenails. Her nipples were pale pink. And the way she was hunkered down like that, the lips of her vagina had opened, and that was pale pink, too. You never saw anything so sexy and so pretty in your life.

"She unfastened my big heavy cowboy belt, and tugged open the studs of my jeans. I was wearing red-and-white striped boxer shorts underneath, and my cock was sticking out like a tentpole. She didn't pull my shorts down right away, she slipped one hand up each leg. She took hold of my balls in one hand, and the shaft of my cock in the other, and she gave me two or three slow, long rubs.

"She said, 'There—you can't make out I don't turn you on. You're as wet as me.' As a matter of fact the whole head of my cock was slippery with juice, and she massaged it and smoothed it up and down until I had to run my fingers into her hair and tell her to stop, otherwise the session would have ended right then and there with me creaming my shorts.

"She pulled down my shorts, and then she got me back for licking *her* by licking *me*—just the very end of my cock, so that when she lifted her head there was a thin shining string of juice joining the tip of her tongue and the end of my cock. She licked it, and then she laughed, and I knew that we were going to have a great time. She'd never done anything like that to me before, not in the middle of the afternoon, in the bathroom, with all the lights on. It all seemed so relaxed and perfect and right. I guess we were discovering each other again. Well—maybe more than that. I guess we were discovering each other for the first time."

In the tub or shower, you and your partner can soap each other, massage each other, kiss and caress each other. Of course you can stroke each other's genitalia, but this is a time when it's important not to rush things—and very important for the man to resist the temptation to make love to his partner or to encourage her to bring him to a climax.

Mutual soaping and washing should be performed as a ritual of closeness and care. Quite apart from that, it's a very sensual experience.

"Jerry had never washed me before, not completely. He's washed my back, of course, when I was sitting in the tub. But he'd never stood naked in the same shower-stall and soaped me and washed me all over. He was fascinated by the sensation of soaping and washing my breasts. I have quite large breasts, and he found that smoothing and massaging soap all over them really turned him on. He held them in his hands as if he were weighing them, and then he smeared soap all over my nipples, and washed them around and around. He lifted them up to the shower-jet, to rinse them, and then he took them between his lips, and sucked them gently up against the roof of his mouth.

"At the same time I was holding his penis, which was totally rigid, and gently rubbing my hand up and down it. But after a few moments he said, 'Stop, you're going to have to stop.' And when I lifted his penis, I saw that there was a single white drop of sperm sliding from the end of it. It looked like a necklace with a single pearl on it. He must have been right on the very brink of coming. He had to switch the shower to cold for a second, and we both shouted out and laughed like crazy."

That was twenty-nine-year-old Ruth, a grade-school teacher from Venice, California. It's interesting that she highlights the *exploratory* nature of the Mutual Discovery Session—the fact that it gives lovers the freedom to investigate each other's minds and bodies. This is Netta, a twenty-five-year-old editorial assistant from New York City: "John and I were always pretty sensual together—you know, very physical people. But I guess we had some underlying problems in our relationship which we hadn't faced up to when we first dated. A lot of them were connected with the fact that I'm black and he's white. It's not that either of us are prejudiced in any way at all, but I come from a background where we didn't get close to too many whites, and John originally came from a town in Minnesota where they didn't see a black face from one year's end to the next. We were strongly attracted toward each other from the very start, but as time went by we allowed our differences to alienate us.

"But, you know, when we decided to spend that time rediscovering each other, everything changed, right from the moment we undressed each other and stepped into that shower. John couldn't take his eyes off me, couldn't take his hands off me. He treated me the way he should have treated me right from the start, like a lady, rather than just a girl he wanted to take to bed.

"Usually I shave my head, and wear different wigs to the office. John washed my scalp and he kissed me and he said, 'It's like I've opened my eyes and looked at you for the first time since I first saw you. I've been taking you for granted, but not any more.'

"I didn't know what to say back, but he washed me all over, and he said, 'Look at that, white soap on black skin. It's beautiful.' He loves my nipples, because they're so black, and because they stick out so much, even when I'm not cold or anything. And he likes me to stay real thin, which I do anyway, for my own pride. He says he likes to see a triangle of space between a woman's thighs, especially mine.

"He soaped in between my legs, and held me close while he did it. The feeling of that was so sensual. He held my cunt in his hand like he was holding a small bird or something, gently soaping me all the time. But then his middle finger slipped right up inside me, and that felt so good. I could have stayed in that shower all day, with the warm water pouring over us, and John's finger sliding in and out of my cunt, all soapy and slippery. He slipped another finger inside and opened me up wider, and I rested my head on his shoulder and felt like I was in heaven.

"Then he did something he'd never done before. He took one of his fingers out of my cunt and soaped it some more, and then he pushed it very slowly up my ass. I tightened up at first, I didn't know what to think, but he said, 'Ssh, enjoy it. Don't tighten up, push against me.' I didn't understand what he meant at first, but then I pushed my ass-muscles *against* his finger, and he could slip it in easily, right up to the knuckle.

"At first I didn't know whether I liked the sensation or not. I guess I was surprised and embarrassed, too. But then he began to work his finger around and around in my ass, probing deeper and deeper, and I began to feel this tightening-up sensation between my legs. I found that I was biting John's shoulder, and I was all tense, and all the time his finger kept working around and around.

"I could feel his cock up against my bare stomach, bobbing hard against me every time his finger circled around. I took hold of it and held it tight, and I could hear John breathing deeper and deeper.

"I couldn't reach an orgasm, I was too tense. But after a while John said, 'Turn off the shower,' which I did. He didn't take out his finger, though. He didn't even take it out when he picked me up in his arms and carried me out of the shower and out of the bathroom and all wet into the bedroom.

"I was saying, 'I'm all wet, I'm all wet! The bed's going to be drenched!' But John said, 'It doesn't matter, take a look.' And he laid me back and opened up my legs, and said, 'Look, we're joined,' and there was his finger so white and my ass clenched around it so black. He slid his finger out, and back in again, and out, and back in again, and each time it felt strange but beautiful, and I guess we both learned something then, that we could be totally one, no matter what color we were, no matter what people thought about us."

In the tub or in the shower, lovers can metaphorically wash away the inhibitions and the hardened attitudes that may have been causing them sexual difficulties. They can renew their closeness, renew their physical contact, and try to look at each other with completely fresh eyes.

We have already touched on several important discussion points in the revival of your sex life . . . such as oral sex, anal sex, mutual masturbation and pubic shaving. The reason why these points are so important is that (in that same order) they were the

Top Five quoted by most men as sexual variations which they believed could instantly and radically improve their relationship—if only the women in their lives would try them.

They also happen to be the Top Five of sexual variations which women are most cautious about trying. Many women, for instance, have said that they do occasionally enjoy anal sex, particularly as an alternative to lovemaking during their period, or when they're feeling "very raunchy indeed." But there are almost as many women who don't like being anally penetrated, especially by a fully-erect penis.

However, we can deal with all of these variations later. Right now, you've showered and toweled, and you should be more than ready to begin the next stage of your Mutual Discovery Session . . . the session that will eventually encourage both of you to think nothing at all of making love every single day of the week.

Rediscovering the ins and outs of your partner's body (and how it responds) are essential to the revival or the expansion of your love life.

But it's surprising how many lovers don't know very much about their partners' bodies . . . and even more surprising how many don't know very much about their own.

If a man has been brought up without women in his family (sisters, or an unabashed mother), or if a woman has been brought up without men in her family, it can be quite possible for him or her not to have a pinsharp idea of what the opposite sex looks like.

In fact, I tried a fascinating experiment. I asked all of the men and women who contributed to this book to draw me the most accurate and complete picture they could of both male and female genitalia.

From my long experience of sexual counseling, I wasn't particularly surprised when it became clear that even some men and women who had been married for years (even some who had been married several times) had an extremely limited idea of what their partner's "private parts" looked like.

Obviously, because so much of them is normally concealed from open view, men had difficulty in drawing an accurate picture of their lovers' vulvas. But almost as many women had only the vaguest notion of what their *own* genitalia looked like, and drew them as little more than a slit. "I've never really examined them," was the reply I was given, time and time again.

And this despite the fact that physical self-knowledge is the very first step to happier and more frequent lovemaking.

Fortunately, the Mutual Discovery Session can help both of you simultaneously to make the closer acquaintance of your sexuality, both physical and emotional.

Now that you're in that warm comfortable environment together, you can begin to explore each other's bodies. Some of you may like to put on a little mood music at this time, but it's essential that the music doesn't distract or disturb you in any way. Similarly, some of you may like to play an erotic video on your television with the sound turned down. But unless your love life is already quite active, and you're using the Mutual Discovery Session more as a way of widening your erotic horizons than as a master-class in lovemaking, it's probably better to leave the TV screen blank just for the moment.

You see, the most important thing of all now is

not to rush. You have all the time you need. Take things slowly, and at the end of the session you'll have become physically closer to your lover than you could have imagined possible.

The greatest complaint that most women have about their partners' lovemaking is that it's "all over in seconds." It's hardly surprising after months or years of "whip-it-in-and-whip-it-out" intercourse that many women begin to feel as if, sexually, they're about as significant to their partners as an inflatable doll.

So . . . make him take it *slowly!*

Kissing is the first priority. You can lie on the bed, futon, sofa, or floor together and learn how to kiss all over again. Pretend you've just met. Pretend you're in high school. Hold each other in your arms and kiss each other as if this is the very first time you've ever done it.

Run your tongues around each other's lips and teeth and tongues. Take it in turns to explore inside each other's mouths. Take it slowly, savor it, appreciate it. Ask each other how they most like to be kissed. Forget about the fact that you're naked, and you're beginning to feel like having intercourse. You're not allowed to do that until later.

Some women like to have their ears kissed and nuzzled, others hate it. Does your partner know whether you like it or not? Have you *told* him? There are all kinds of caresses which can gradually arouse you and bring your whole body and mind into a highly erotic state, but unless you tell your lover what they are, he's never going to know.

It's conceivable, of course, that you haven't yet found them all yourself. Apart from your ears and your back, you have erotically-sensitive nerves just on top of your pelvis, inside your thighs, behind your knees. And it's amazing how erotic it is to have your feet massaged.

Your lover should trail his fingertips all over you . . . *except* in those really intimate places. He should kiss you wherever he feels like it, and if any of his kisses give you one of those really special frissons of delight, make sure that he's aware of it. If your sexual relationship doesn't satisfy you largely because you've failed to tell your lover what touches and kisses excite you the most, then I'm afraid that you're just as much to blame as he is, if not more so.

Now you should explore your lover's body yourself, using fingers and tongue and even teeth if you're careful. Try nuzzling and biting his neck and shoulders (although make sure you don't leave any hickeys that are likely to show over his collar when he turns up for work tomorrow—and don't leave any at all if he's married to somebody else—that's straightforward sexual eitquette).

You can rake your fingernails lightly all the way from his shoulders down his back and around to the sides of his hips—a caress which, if you hit the right nerves, should give him a shudder of pleasure.

Ignore his penis at this time, even if it's pretty hard to ignore, and continue with that softly-scratching caress around the sides of his thighs, behind his knees, and down the backs of his calves.

Although you're keeping genital caresses for later, you can heighten both his level of arousal and yours by "accidentally" brushing your breasts against his back, or "accidentally" touching his penis with your arm or your thigh.

After your light scratching caresses, kiss your way back up to his chest again, licking around his nipples, and taking them gently in between your teeth and nipping them. But not *too* hard. His nipples are just as sensitive as yours, and you can almost instantaneously cause an angry or aggrieved reaction by chewing his nipples too enthusiastically.

Neither of you should forget caresses of the scalp and the hair which can induce a wonderful drowzy eroticism and a great sense of sexual peace and well-being. Caressing his hair can also lead you very naturally and smoothly into the next stage of the Mutual Discovery Session . . . which is the discovery of your lover's genitalia.

Getting to know your lover's body in intimate detail is not only arousing in itself but critical to your ability to improve your love life. When you know just how his penis works and how it reacts to your caresses, you will be capable of stimulating it in all kinds of different ways . . . and the more ways you know, the more you will encourage him to make love to you more often.

Let's put it like this: if you know a dozen different ways of arousing him, then you can make love to him six days a week for two weeks and never have to use the same technique twice.

You will probably be more familiar with the external appearance of your lover's genitalia than either of you are with yours. After all, an erect penis is hardly one of those things that you can fail to notice. But all the same, you may not be aware how it works internally, and how much you can control those workings—for his pleasure and to your advantage.

It's preferable in your Mutual Discovery Session for you to discover your lover's sexual organs first, since his discovery of yours will almost inevitably lead to the first stages of lovemaking, and the aim is to make the session as slow and as relaxed as possible, giving you both plenty of time to discuss (and display) your sexual responses.

I mentioned that caressing his hair can lead you naturally to this next stage of your sexual exploration. You can do this by kissing him and trailing your own hair against his face and neck, and then kissing your way down his chest, around his hips, until you are face to face with his penis. If you have long hair, you will probably discover that he adores the sensation of having his penis wound around and tickled with your hair. In fact, twenty-one-year-old Christina, from Dallas, Texas, reported that her thirty-seven-year-old lover Steve absolutely adored being aroused by her long blonde hair.

"It first started when I was kissing his cock. I kissed the head of it, and then I kissed and licked the underneath of the shaft, you know, and went right down and kissed his balls. Of course his cock got all tangled up in my hair. I reached up with my hand to rub his cock while I was kissing and licking his balls, and of course when I rubbed it it was all wrapped around with hair. I heard him say something like, 'That feels too good to be true.' I had one of his balls in my mouth, and I felt it really tighten. The next thing I knew he was shooting great loads of warm sperm into my hair. He really likes it, it really turns him. I guess part of it is because I'm so much younger than him, and his ex-wife used to have really short hair. But I know lots of men like it. Steve says it feels like nothing else: silky and scratchy at the same time, that's what he calls it."

Your lover's penis will probably be erect by now—although don't be disenchanted if it isn't. Your first Mutual Discovery Session will be a new and unfamiliar and even daunting time for both of you, especially if you haven't been used to sharing your sexual desires very closely.

The head of your lover's penis is called the *glans*.

As you can see it is curved and rather wedge-shaped, with an opening, or *meatus*, through which your lover both urinates and ejaculates semen. Just below the opening is a thin line or web of skin called the *frenum*, which as a matter of interest is Latin for "bridle."

The opening itself is extremely sensitive to *gentle* caresses. Part it carefully with your fingers and you will probably see that it is welling up already with that clear lubricating fluid which indicates that your lover is aroused. Taste the fluid with the tip of your tongue and you will find that it has a faint but distinctive aroma, and also that it is remarkably slippery. A tiny drop can lubricate the whole of the glans.

The frenum is also highly sensitive, and your lover will find that a quick, light, circular caressing of the frenum and the opening of his penis with your fingertip is highly erotic—particularly if there is a little fluid on your fingertip to lubricate it. If there isn't, you can use either saliva or (more excitingly) some of the lubricating fluid from your own vagina.

Around the glans is a ridge called the *corona*. The shape of the glans and the prominence of the corona varies quite considerably from one man to another. Some men have plum-shaped glans, others have wedge-shaped glans, some have such prominent coronas that their glans is shaped almost like a duck's bill.

It doesn't matter what shape your lover's glans is, as long as you like it. It's important to remember that genitalia of both sexes is as varied as their faces. All cocks and all cunts are *not* alike. For centuries there have been all kinds of old wives' tales about how you can tell the size of a man's penis by looking at his nose or the size of his ears, but I'm afraid that's about as unreliable a guide as trying to tell the size of a woman's nipples by looking at her eyes.

The glans is an expansion of the tissue which runs up the center of your lover's penis, the *corpus spongiosum* or spongy tissue. Although this tissue becomes stiffer when your lover has an erection, it always remains reasonably soft and spongy, allowing sperm to shoot along his urethra and out through his opening when he reaches a climax.

If you squeeze the shaft of his erect penis quite tightly, you will feel the *corpora cavernosa*, two "caverns" which make up most of the shaft. They divide at the base of the penis and are attached to the pubic bone. When your lover is sexually excited, these "caverns" fill up with blood, and his penis becomes erect. Muscular tightening restricts the return of the blood to the main bloodstream, thus keeping his penis erect.

While you're handling your lover's penis, there are some interesting points to discover and discuss. Most men, when they are being masturbated by hand, prefer you to hold their penises quite high up—just below the corona. But ask your lover to show you which grip he finds the most pleasurable so that the next time you want to masturbate him you'll know exactly how.

Handling your lover's penis with familiarity and confidence will make you a much more skillful lover. You should get to know it as intimately as you can . . . just as he will be getting to know your genitals intimately.

You will find that if your partner has difficulties in keeping up an erection (particularly if he's tired, or had too much to drink) you can assist in keeping him stiff by gripping the shaft of his penis right down at the base, next to his body, and squeezing it. This will

help to keep the blood in his corpora cavernosa—
and partially maintain his stiffness. With luck, the
continuing friction of his still-swollen glans inside
your vagina will help him to regain his natural hard-
on.

Another important penis-handling technique is
the "squeeze technique" which was introduced with
astonishing success by the sex-therapists Masters
and Johnson. Its primary purpose is to help men
suffering from premature ejaculation—coming too
soon—but it can also be used to extend your lovemaking for fifteen or twenty minutes before your
lover eventually ejaculates.

What you have to do is hold his penis between
your thumb and the first two fingers of the same
hand. You place your thumb on his frenum—that
little line of skin where the shaft ends and the head
of the penis begins. Then you place your two fingers on the opposite side of the penis, one on each
side of the corona, or ridge.

If your lover is feeling an irresistible urge to climax, arrange between you that he should take out
his penis and that you should then hold it in the
way I've described and squeeze it fairly hard for a
slow count of three. Your lover will lose his urge
to ejaculate, although his erection will also soften
a little (nobody quite knows why). But if you then
wait for fifteen to thirty seconds, you will be able
to massage him back to erection, and carry on.

If he feels the urge to ejaculate yet again, you
can perform the squeeze yet again—and again, and
again, and again—until *you're* satisfied, too. When
your lover finally does ejaculate, his climax should
be extremely intense and pleasurable.

The advantage of knowing these penis-handling
techniques is that you can tremendously improve
your sex-life *yourself*, without the need for therapy

or professional guidance. If your lover has been coming too quickly, you will obviously be feeling less-than-satisfied, and in a close sexual relationship there is no way that you can hide your dissatisfaction. If it hasn't happened already, your lover will sense your frustration, and this will make him feel even more inadequate than he does already.

When a man feels sexually inadequate (no matter how unjustified that feeling may be), the result is inevitably whole or partial impotence, and very much less than six-days-a-week sex for you.

If you're unsure of the "squeeze," try it out now by masturbating your lover until he's right on the brink of ejaculation, then s–q–u–e–e–z–e. Don't be afraid to do it hard—the erect penis is incredibly tough. In fact, there's a famous holy man in Nepal who is capable of hanging twelve cinderblocks halfway along the shaft of his erect penis, and the last I heard he was still in good working order.

Your lover may be circumcized or he may still have his foreskin. The arguments about the pros and cons of circumcision are still going on, but there are signs that it is not so universally accepted as it used to be—except, of course, in some religions.

If your lover still retains his foreskin, it will of course peel back as his penis stiffens, exposing the glans in the same way that a circumcized penis does. There is no reliable evidence to suggest that circumcized men have less-sensitive penises than uncircumcized men; or that they suffer more frequently from premature ejaculation. Some years ago, it was suggested that the wives of circumcized men were less prone to cervical cancer than the wives of uncircumcized men, presumably on the grounds that uncircumcized men find it more difficult to keep their penises clean. This suggestion was unreliable to say the least—although I do emphasize the need for both of you to have a very high standard of sexual hygiene. You can help your lover now and again by washing his penis for him . . . and making sure you take your time.

4

Your Lover's Body: Part Two

A question that I'm asked more than any other (and just as frequently by women as by men) is "how big should a penis be?"

Like every other part of the anatomy, penises vary enormously in size, and if you've seen any porno videos or magazines, you will have probably seen one or two penises which, when erect, are staggeringly large, like that of the late John Holmes. But while a huge penis may look impressive, it's of no special advantage when it comes to sex.

An interesting experience was had in this respect by eighteen-year-old Laura, from Las Vegas, Nevada: "When I first came to work in Las Vegas, I started to date a guy called Eddy, who was originally from Oregon. He was a terrific-looking guy; he used to work out a lot, and he had a really muscular chest and narrow hips. He looked like a logger or something, especially when he used to wear his plaid shirts and his faded jeans. In fact he looked so much like a logger that a lot of guys used to think he was gay. I can tell you for sure, though—no way was Eddy gay. He was a real sweet guy, too. He didn't have too much money, and he was living in a rented trailer just outside of town. We dated quite a few times before he took me back there and we made love together. I'll never forget when he undressed. His body was real tanned and muscular with a flat stomach and a really small tight ass. He didn't wear any underwear, and you should have seen the cock that came out of the front of his jeans. He had short blond pubic hair, and then this huge cock, thick and stiff, with a massive great crimson head on it. He said his cock was ten inches once when he measured it, but it looked like more. I thought I'd never get it inside me.

"I stripped down to just my panties, and I knelt on the bed and took hold of his cock and I couldn't believe it. It was like a horse's cock. I kissed him, and I rubbed his cock up and down a few times. Then I went down on him, and licked all around that huge crimson head, and it was delicious. He tasted like sweat and jeans and pee, a real man's taste, it always turns me on. I took the whole head of his cock in my mouth, and it almost choked me, it was so big. But I thought: what a way to die, choked by the biggest cock in the world.

"I sucked him and rubbed him, and then he pushed me back on the bed, and pulled my panties to one side, and guided his cock up to my pussy. I looked up at him and said, 'It won't be too big, will it? How am I going to get it all in?' But he just smiled and said, 'Hold yourself open.'

"I pulled my pussy-lips apart, and stretched my legs as wide as I could. I couldn't resist looking down and watching it. He slipped two fingers halfway inside me, so that they were all juicy, and then he massaged the juice all over the head of his cock so that it was shining. Then he slowly pushed himself in. I could see the head burying itself in my pussy, and then the shaft, with its huge bulging veins, and when he got about halfway in I could feel him inside me, I could feel him right up inside my pussy, stretching me wide open. I can remember that I was gasping all the time. But he took hold of my shoulders, and with one last push he was right up inside me, blond pubic hair right up against brown pubic hair.

"He was what you might call a good straightforward fuck. He never got tired. I used to lie there on that bed in the trailer with the sun coming through the blinds, my legs wide apart, and let him push that huge cock in and out of me as long as he wanted. He was so strong, too. He could fuck me standing up. I used to cling on to him, naked, and slide slowly down, so that his massive cock went further up inside me than anything ever went before. He could walk around the trailer carrying me, with his cock still up inside me.

"But—I don't know—he was big, but he wasn't what you might call *sensual*. He'd just push in and out, in and out. He never gave me a climax, although I did have climaxes. I used to diddle myself while he was fucking me, and he didn't mind. In fact he quite liked it because my pussy used to squeeze his cock when I finally came. I liked to suck him a lot because his cock was superb. I remember one time we hadn't seen each other for a week, and we went straight back to the trailer. We stripped off and I had to have his cock in my mouth like *immediately*, I wanted him that bad. I knelt down in front of him, and I took his cock as far down as I could. It crammed up my whole mouth, almost down my throat. I rubbed him and licked him and sucked him, and then I suddenly felt him tense up. I grabbed hold of the cheeks of that lovely tight ass of his and pulled him in and out of my mouth, quicker and quicker, with my tongue flicking the head of his cock faster and faster, too. He grabbed my shoulders and he shot his whole load into my mouth, most of it straight down my throat, but the rest of it all smothering my tongue and my lips. I took his cock out of my mouth and gave it a squeeze, and a big drop of sperm came out of it, and dripped down on to my breast. 'S'posed to make your breasts grow,' he said. 'You don't want them uneven,' and he squeezed some more sperm on to my other breast. He lay down on the bed and I went on licking and sucking his cock even though it was soft. I couldn't get enough of the taste of it, the lovely weight of it, it was so big. I rubbed it all over my face and kissed it and kissed it. And I knew then that I'd never go out with Eddy again. He didn't have the first idea about how to please me, how to turn me on. The only pleasure I was getting out of sex with Eddy was pleasure that I was making for myself. I might just as well have been masturbating with a huge ten-inch vibrator, do you know what I mean? He was just a cock with a man on the end. All right, a huge cock. An enormous cock. And I guess the size of his cock was part of his sexual problem. Girls just gasped when they saw it, and said 'Giggle-giggle, how on earth am I going to get all of *that* inside me?' and Eddy thought that was all he had to do. Like he never went down on me once, and I must have sucked him a hundred times.

"After Eddy I went out with this really quiet guy called Paul. He'd come to Vegas to work out some accountancy problem. He was good-looking, for sure, but he wasn't a tree-chopper like Eddy, and I guess he was six or seven years older. He used to wear these really smart lightweight suits and prescription Ray-Bans, and he looked pretty cool.

"The first night he took me out he gave me dinner at his hotel. Then we went up to his room for a nightcap. He didn't act too suave, you know. I mean he wasn't too smooth. But he took real good care of me, opening the door for me, stuff like that, and that made me feel real feminine. He had a bottle of champagne on ice. I'll never forget that. I'd never drunk champagne before. And—well—to cut a long story short, we ended up in bed together.

"He wasn't at all like Eddy, not physically. He was really lean and dark, with dark hair on his chest. He looked fit. He said he played squash. But he didn't have a huge bulging chest, and he sure didn't have the other thing that Eddy had. We knelt on the bed together, undressing each other, and when I reached into Paul's shorts and took out his cock . . . well, I'd be lying if I said that I wasn't disappointed. Especially after Eddy's monster.

"I bent down and took his cock into my mouth right away. It seemed thin and small compared with Eddy's. I guess I went down on him so quick because I thought he wasn't going to be able to satisfy me, and I might as well make the best of it. But he took hold of my face in his hands and kissed me, and said, 'There's plenty of time for that.'

"We lay on the bed together and he totally took charge. He kissed me, he stroked me, he played with my nipples. Then gradually *he* went down on *me*, which was something that had never happened to me before. He kissed all around my pussy, and then he ran his tongue down it and used his tongue to open up my lips. I could feel him licking my clitoris and probing further down, and then waggling his tongue inside my pussy.

"He gave me such feelings, you don't have any idea. He licked me until I didn't know where I was or what I was supposed to be doing. Suddenly I felt like somebody was drawing the sheets out from under me, and I started to jump. I didn't realize it, but he was giving me a climax.

"I felt as if I'd had enough. I mean I just wanted to lie there and think about what had happened to me. Paul didn't stop there. He lay down beside me right away, no hesitation, and lifted my leg, and slid his cock up into me. It went in real easy, of course, because I was so slippery, but although his cock was smaller than Eddy's, it touched all the right spots in just the same way. Better, in fact, because he had a way of pushing it just at that certain angle that felt fantastic.

"At the same time he started playing with my clitoris with one hand, flicking it so light at first that I could hardly feel it, but then quicker and harder. He cupped my bottom with his other hand and kept on stroking me right between my legs with his fingertips and touching us where we joined. Before I knew what was happening, I had another climax. I'd never had two like that before, one after the other, and then Paul climaxed, too.

"I thought he'd finished, but he hadn't. He went down on me again, and licked me some more. I couldn't manage another climax, but after a while he came up the bed and kissed me, and his mouth was all wet with the taste of both of us together, my juice and his sperm, and I kissed him and licked him until he was all dry.

"You ask me about men with big cocks? And I say, it doesn't make any difference, and that's for real."

An average-sized penis measures between 2¾–4½ inches when soft; and between 4½–8¼ inches when erect. The circumference averages 3–4½ inches when soft, and 3¾–4¾ inches when erect. These days, penis size is medically measured by volume rather than by length and circumference. This indicates the filling capacity of the penis in relation to a woman's vagina. A good average volume is between 5.7 inches ^{3}–28.8 inches^3.

Without the proper laboratory equipment, it's a

little difficult for your lover to measure the volume of his own penis, but you should be reassured that your vagina is so elastic that *any* penis can give you all of the pleasure that you deserve. Problems with smaller penises only arise when men are worried that they aren't going to be able to satisfy their partners—with the result that they can manage only partial erection or no erection at all.

Now you can take a close look at your lover's balls, or *testes*. Although you obviously can't explore all of his internal workings, it's surprising how much you will be able to feel and how that will help you to understand male sexuality. There is one strict rule, though, for exploring your lover's balls: treat them like the rare eggs they are. Any squeezing will hurt like hell and may bring your Mutual Discovery Session to an immediate and unplanned-for end.

You will be able to feel the testes themselves. They are usually about two inches in length, an inch in breadth and 1¼ inch in width. They are surrounded by various tough coverings to protect them. Each of them contains about 250 glandular lobes in which spermatazoa are produced.

The spermatazoa are collected up by a small mass of convoluted tubes which you can feel behind the balls. This structure is called the *epididymis*, which is Greek for "on top of the twins"—referring to where it sits, behind each of the twinned testicles. From the tail of the epididymis, spermatazoa are sent on their way along the *vas deferens*, or spermatic duct, which you should be able to feel deep between your lover's legs.

The spermatic duct takes the spermatazoa up inside his body to his *seminal vesicles*—two strangely rubber-glove-shaped organs which are double-parked between his bladder and his rectum. You won't be able to feel these of course, but they're crucially important. They supply most of the fluid that makes up semen.

Once the spermatazoa and the seminal fluid have joined, they are carried to a small bulb-shaped reservoir, and there they patiently wait for *you* to arouse your lover to the point of ejaculation. At that moment, the semen is shot out along his urethra in convulsive bursts and spurts out of his penis.

But don't try doing that just yet. There's plenty of time.

One of the most vexed questions that I have to deal with is that of how much semen a man should normally ejaculate. So many erotic books describe men shooting out gallons of semen with each ejaculation (and being capable almost immediately of shooting out even *more* gallons of semen) that many men become worried when they ejaculate little more than a generous teaspoonful that they are sexually inadequate.

Arlene, a twenty-seven-year-old ranch wife from Wyoming, wrote me: "Does the amount of jissom that a man produces in any way tally with how much he loves the woman he's making love to? Because I've always read in stories about men producing so much that a girl's whole mouth is filled right up to bursting, or filling up her pussy. But my Gil can only manage such a small amount, and I'm concerned that he doesn't truly care for me, but is just pretending."

The only way in which the amount of semen which your lover produces could possibly be related to how much he loves you is if he's recently made love to another woman . . . and, believe me, this is an extremely difficult and unreliable way of finding out!

The fact is that after about two days of sexual continence, the average man ejaculates no more than .07–0.21 fluid ounces (2–6ml). That's about enough to fill a teaspoon to overflowing.

Of course, you'll have noticed that semen is extremely viscous, and that it can appear to cover an area that is way out of proportion to the amount that has actually been ejaculated. That's one reason why some people imagine that men shoot out far more than they actually do.

The other reason is that how much semen a man ejaculates is often taken (completely mistakenly) as a measure of his virility. ("My God! What a man! He ejaculated 0.27 fluid ounces of semen!") Every pornographic story you may care to pick up describes the same fantasy of vast oceans of sperm.

Here's a typical example from a recently-published but anonymous story titled "A Sex Machine Called Tina": "Then I took the head of his cock back into my mouth and I started to suck, suck harder, and the glans grew hot and swollen and the taste and feel of that prick was (sic) so very good that my climaxes were already beginning.

"Then he jerked, and his glans grew bigger and he started to cum, and his spunk was thick, and there was a lot of it. He was giving me lots and lots of very tasty spunk in my mouth and I was drinking it down, taking it down my throat just as fast as he was pumping it into my sucking mouth.

"Yes, there was a lot of it, and I was very pleased with him, and he was still shooting out sperm, so I took his prick from my mouth and let the rest of it go all over my chin and cheek."

That genuine and very typical excerpt just goes to show you that many of the people who write pornographic fiction are as unsure of their sexual facts as they are of their basic grammar. For sure, there's no harm in *fantasizing* about huge quantities of sperm; but the truth is very different. So don't be disappointed if your lover seems to be producing something short of a U.S. pint!

I've come across couples several times in the past twenty years who make a point of saving the man's semen for a week or two—sometimes even longer—for the express purpose of using it in sex play at a later date.

I first heard about this erotic variation when I was working in Stockholm in the 1970s. Since then it has come up again and again, in different ways, and obviously expresses a man's desire to be able to produce more semen during lovemaking, and a woman's enjoyment of it.

Here's Annetta, a thirty-three-year-old home-maker from Los Angeles, California: "I know that there are many women who don't enjoy oral sex. Many of my friends think that the whole idea of taking a man's penis into your mouth is absolutely revolting. But for some reason I've always adored it. My first experience of sex was sucking a senior boy's cock at high school, and I swallowed his sperm because he shot it straight down my throat and I simply wasn't ready for it. I've always found the taste of sperm a turn-on. I actually think it's the best taste in the world, second to strawberries. Or maybe it's as good as strawberries. I have tested it out! I was eating strawberries in bed one Saturday morning, and my husband was lying next to me, and I was rubbing his cock. When he started to come, I had a brilliant idea. I held his cock over my plate of strawberries so that they were all topped with sperm. I ate them like that and they were delicious. Sperm goes better with strawberries than sugar or pepper. Strawberries-and-cream, I called it!

"Anyhow, what I sometimes do is masturbate Leonard in the early morning, before he gets up for work, and I collect his sperm in a glass jelly jar. I keep the jar in the icebox, and when it's about half-full, I take it out and let it warm up by the fire.

"When we make love in front of the fire, I take the lid off the jelly jar and dip my fingers into it, and lubricate my cunt with it, so I'm real juicy right from the start. I love the smell of it, it's so strong and musky! Sometimes I pour some over my breasts, too: and Leonard massages my nipples with his own sperm.

"We make love, and we're all slippery and messy, but I love it. I feel like I really belong to him. I can smear sperm all around his balls and in between the cheeks of his ass, and then I can slide two or three fingers right up inside his ass, sometimes four, and feel right up inside him. I don't usually climax when we're actually making love, but after he's finished, Leonard spreads my legs wide and goes down on me and licks my cunt. My favorite thing then is to scoop the last of his sperm out of the jelly-jar and swallow it down in handfuls. Then lick my fingers, to taste the last of it!

"Sometimes, when he's away on business, I save his sperm before he goes, and then drink it while he's away, while I masturbate."

Of course there's absolutely nothing wrong with your sexual urges if you don't relish semen as much as Annetta. Some women simply don't like the taste of it at all, and many are put off by its "raw-egg" consistency. It's up to their lovers to be understanding. But there are of course many compromises which are just as erotic and fulfilling as the swallowing of semen. You can take your lover's penis out of your mouth just before he ejaculates, and aim his spurting semen over your vulva, or over your breasts, or over your face.

Swallowing semen—even in large quantities—is completely harmless. It is only a combination of proteins and simple sugars. Several women have claimed that, swallowed regularly, it has the effect of enlarging their breasts, but I regret that I have to regard that claim with considerable skepticism. If it *really* had that effect, millions of women would be fellating their lovers night and day.

You have almost completed your exploration of your lover's sexual parts. Only his anus remains.

Many women seem to have the idea that a man who enjoys having a finger or a vibrator or anything else pushed into his rectum has secret homosexual tendencies. But the fact is that the anus is richly endowed with erotically-stimulating nerves which a woman can stimulate just as excitingly as another man, and that anal sex between happy and stable heterosexuals has been busily going on throughout recorded history.

We shall be talking about anal sex in more detail later—particularly as it relates to more frequent lovemaking—but for the time being all you need to do to bring this particular phase of your Mutual Discovery Session to a close is to explore your lover's ass with one finger.

You will need a little lubricant (the juice from your own vagina is the most natural and the most effective; but KY Jelly or any slippery cream will do, provided it doesn't contain any perfumes that might irritate or sting). You will also need reasonably well-trimmed nails. They don't have to be cut down to the bone, if you promise to be careful, but they shouldn't be movie-star daggers, either. Not unless you want to send your lover into orbit with your first probe.

There's also one reassuring thing you may need to know: the rectum is usually empty, and so anal probing won't be dirty or offensive. The rectum *does* harbor some pretty feisty bacteria, however, so as much as you enjoy anal sex, *never* insert your fingers into your vagina after probing his ass; and *never* let him do the same.

Gently open your lover's thighs as far as they will go, so that his anus is exposed to your view. Touch it with your fingertip and you will see that it automatically tightens. In time, your lover will learn to react differently when you touch him, and his anus will actually open (or *dilate*) to let you in, just as yours will do the same for him. This is one way in which doctors who are treating women for persistent vaginal infections can tell if they are having regular anal intercourse . . . even though the women themselves may strenuously deny it.

Now push your lubricated finger slowly into his anus. You can lightly cup and caress his balls at the same time, in order to increase his pleasure, or even circle your fingertip around the opening of his cock, although you should be careful not to bring him to a climax yet. You haven't had your turn yet!

At first, the grip of his anal muscles might be so tight that you feel you won't be able to push your finger in further than half-an-inch. But if you withdraw it a little, then push again, turning as you push, you will eventually find that your finger is past the muscular ring, and actually inside the rectum.

You can slowly churn your finger around, massaging the walls of the rectum. They will feel soft and slippery—very similar to the walls of your vagina. The rectum (Latin for "straight") is about five inches long, and it can fairly easily accommodate an erect penis or a vibrator, although in doing so it probably exceeds its natural limits.

It's possible that either you or your lover may

have negative feelings about anal stimulation. But if you try it occasionally, you will find that it adds a new dimension to your lovemaking. Women very rarely think of penetrating their lovers anally, even though the experience (for a man) can be devastatingly erotic. A rotating, "beckoning" gesture, particularly if you can manage to do it with two fingers, will put rhythmic pressure on his prostatic utricle (the small sac in which his semen is stored) and on the deeply-buried base of the spongy tissue which makes up the main shaft of his penis.

To have his penis hand-rubbed or gently licked and sucked to climax while you are stimulating his rectum will give your lover an experience he will never forget . . . and which he will want to repeat as soon as possible.

If you have a vibrator on hand during your Mutual Discovery Session, lubricate it well, and try to insert that into your lover's anus. You can also use a dildo or a vibrator during lovemaking (when you won't be able to reach inside his anus with your fingers). When the vibrator is buried up to the hilt in his bottom, with your hand on the base of it to control its movement, you will find that you can give him extra stimulus of a kind which he may not even have dreamed about.

Even in the course of exploring your lover's basic anatomy and responses, we've managed to explore a whole lot of new ideas and new suggestions for erotic stimuli. That's the fascinating part about sex. No matter how often you do it, no matter how much you discuss it, there's always room for something new.

Now you can begin to see how you can make love six times a week (if not more!) What you may have thought of as an act that had only two or three variations is in fact one of the most varied and challenging activities that two loving people can do together.

I'm not talking about "1,001 Different Sexual Positions", either. In actual fact there are fewer than half-a-dozen really comfortably and arousing sexual positions. You may have bought a copy of the *Kama Sutra*, but I doubt if you or your lover will ever have much fun trying out the "twining position" or the "half-pressed position" or the "splitting of a bamboo."

However, we can talk about the best way to vary your positions later. Right now, it's time for your lover to explore *you* . . . and the erotic possibilities which can arise from that are almost limitless.

5

What You Want Out Of Sex

"Sex always seemed to be something we did in silence," said thirty-four-year-old Loretta, from Memphis, Tennessee. "As soon as Roy wanted to get it on, he didn't say a word. Didn't say how much he loved me, didn't tell me what was going on inside of his head. It was like he couldn't concentrate on sex and speech both at the same time. Or else he was just plain embarrassed to tell me what he was thinking."

Loretta's complaint echoes the feelings of millions of women everywhere. While men may be assertive in their sexual actions, they tend to be extremely reticent when it comes to putting their sexual feelings into words.

Women like to hear how gorgeous they look, how beautiful their breasts are, how much they turn their lovers on. They like to hear it in *words* and they like to hear it *out loud*.

Yet when it comes to making love, an extraordinarily high number of men completely clam up. This abrupt silence often leads their partners to believe that they have retreated inside of their own fantasies—that they are concentrating on their own pleasure alone—and that they are simply using their partners as a means of getting their rocks off.

This is usually far from the truth. But men *do* find it difficult to articulate their feelings when they're making love. Sometimes they're afraid that talking will interrupt the rhythm of their foreplay; sometimes they're afraid of breaking the mood and losing their erection; sometimes they're afraid they might say something ridiculous.

A lot of their reluctance can be traced back to the old problem of sexual vocabulary. Some men find it hard to say to their wives, "Darling, you have the most beautiful cunt (or pussy) in the world." Just as some women find it difficult to say, "I adore your dick."

I've always thought that one of the best remedies for sex-word-shyness is to find yourself a list of all those taboo words and read through them several times. Some of them are funny, some of them are plain vulgar, some of them are close to beautiful. But in the end—once you've read and said them often enough—they completely lose their feeling of being filthy and forbidden.

For instance, the vagina has variously been described throughout history as: cunt, slit, crack, hole, pee-hole, coozy, pussy, twat, bearded clam, beaver, fanny, quim, box, doughnut, snatch, brownie, cherry-pie, cooch, fern, furburger, gash, muff, poontang, tail, nook, happy valley, trench, snapping turtle, Y, minge, front botty, money-box, mousetrap, jelly-roll, garden, hatch, promised land, rattlesnake canyon, scratch.

And, as I mentioned before, many women have their own pet-names for their private parts. I've heard "Sister Joy," "petty-thing," "Mimi," "pant-ie-cave," and—one of my favorites—"my little smile."

The reason I've raised the subject of talking about sex right here is that you should have been talking to your lover throughout your exploration of his body and his senses. *Talking* to him—telling him what you think about the way he looks and the way he feels. Telling him what he smells like, what he tastes like. And *asking* him, too, about his own feelings.

How does he like to be kissed?

How does he like his body to be caressed?

How does he like you to hold his penis?

How does he like you to kiss his penis?

Does he like *this*? Does he like *that*?

And above all—Is there any way in which he would like you to touch him—but which he has never had the nerve to ask you?

Remember, the Mutual Discovery Session is a time when everything and anything goes; a time when you have promised each other that nothing you say and nothing you do—either of you—will give rise to rejection or offense. It's a time for open minds and open bodies. A time for sharing.

More than anything else, it's a time for discarding old inhibitions, reassessing old prejudices, and discovering new horizons. So, *talk*, both of you, and *listen*. And this will especially apply when your lover is exploring you.

Before your lover begins his exploration of you, it's important for you to be relaxed. If you're tense or anxious, a touch that was meant to be arousing can often feel irritating or harsh. So lie back, and breathe deeply. Take a few sips of wine if you want to. Remember that this is the man you love . . . and the man who loves you enough to want to do something positive about making your sex life even better.

This is often an appropriate moment to look through some sexy magazines. Not only will they keep up the mood of general eroticism, they'll give you a chance to look at the bare breasts and exposed genitalia of other women.

And another point to remember: these magazines are designed to appeal to men. So by taking a look at two or three of them, you'll begin to have some idea of what visual images of women turn men on the most.

"I was truly shocked the first time I saw a porn magazine," confessed Sandy, a twenty-five-year-old bank teller from San Diego, California. "My husband brought some home from a business trip to Holland, and I was totally taken aback. They were so bright, you know. So lurid. Nothing left to the imagination whatsoever. There were pictures of naked girls with their legs wide apart, opening up their vaginas with their fingers so that the camera could see right inside. There were pictures of girls with their own fingers up inside them. And they were all smiling, like they were really enjoying it. I think I would have died on the spot if anybody had asked me to stand in front of a camera like that!"

But later: "When my husband went to work, I took out the magazines and looked through them all again. I'm a woman, and pictures of other women with no clothes on don't particularly turn me on. But I was fascinated to see how different all their vaginas were. There were girls with very thin vaginal lips, and girls with very full wavy vaginal lips. There were girls whose mound of venus really bulged out, you know, and whose vaginas were very up front and exposed. Then there were others whose vaginas were nothing more than a thin slit. Some were pigmented quite dark, others were completely pink. Even their clitorises were different.

"Of course I'd seen other girls with no clothes on at school, but I'd never had the chance to sit and stare at another woman's private parts, which is what a porno magazine gives you the chance to do. And, do you know something, I ended up by *not* being shocked at all. In fact I approve of porno magazines. They're only pictures of people, after all, other people. And we're always insatiably curious about other people.

"I think those magazines are really instructional. Apart from being sexy, of course. Well, some of them are downright dirty. But if you think they're downright dirty, you don't have to buy them, do you?"

Sandy also commented on the endless multiplicity of different kinds of breasts. "There were girls with huge breasts. I don't even know how they managed to walk around with them. There were girls with round breasts, pointed breasts, conical breasts, all kinds. And so many different kinds of nipples. Really tiny rosebud ones on the end of enormous breasts. Really wide ones on the end of small breasts. Nipples like the tops of knickerbocker glories. Pink nipples, brown nipples, *black* nipples."

Even today, in an age which is supposed to be sexually frank, very few women have a really clear and complete idea of what their sexual parts look like, and how they work. When they discover themselves for the first time, many women are amazed. After the publication of my last book *Sex Secrets of the Other Woman*, which gave a full description of the differences between women's sexual parts, I received a letter from Joanna, of Indianapolis, Indiana, who said, "For years I have been secretly ashamed of the way my private parts looked. I thought I was especially ugly, and I have always made an effort not to show myself off, first to boyfriends and then to my husband. I was surprised that they weren't put off by the appearance of my vulva, although I rarely gave them the opportunity to see it. I never let my husband kiss me there, ever, not in thirteen years of marriage.

"Then I began to suspect that my husband was becoming overfond of the woman who runs our local tennis club, and I guess in a fit of desperation I bought your book *Sex Secrets of the Other Woman*. I have to tell you that it's not the kind of book that I would normally consider purchasing, but I just didn't know where to turn. I couldn't tell any of my friends, and my sole surviving sister lives in Canada.

"I found some of the book stimulating and much of it instructional. Perhaps I'm a prude but some of the sexual acts that you described were, frankly, disgusting. But I suppose that everybody has the right to do what they like in private. However there were also a great many surprises in it for me. When I read about the variations in women's sexual parts and what they were actually supposed to look like, I actually burst into tears. I went to the mirror as you suggested and examined myself. Then I plucked up the courage and drove to a liquor store where I know they sell men's magazines. I bought two of them, even though I was very embarrassed and the fellow behind the counter gave me a pretty funny look.

"The first centerfold I opened showed a stunning blonde girl with her legs wide open. Her vulva was almost exactly like mine. I have quite long lips, you see, and I always thought they were hideous, almost freakish. Yet here was this young girl with lips just as long as mine, and she had opened them up so that everybody could see inside. And she was obviously proud of herself. And the magazine had obviously thought her sexy enough to put on their center spread.

"I thought of all the years that I had been hiding

myself. I thought of all the pleasure I could have had from showing myself off to my husband. I hadn't even allowed him to give me oral sex!

"I went home and I ran myself a bath and I did what you suggested in your book—I shaved off my pubic hair, all of it, and when my husband came home I greeted him at the door wearing nothing but one of his shirts. I lifted up the shirt and showed him, and said, 'Look.' I had a moment of panic in case I was mistaken, in case I really *was* ugly. But you should have seen the look that came across his face. It was like the sun coming up. That night we had the best sex we'd ever had in thirteen years, and that night I let him kiss and lick my vagina and it was heaven. I don't know whether he'd ever shown any real interest in the woman from the tennis club, but it certainly didn't come to anything, not after that night. Thank you for having the nerve to tell it like it is."

Your lover should start his discovery of you in the same way that you started your discovery of him—by kissing. Tell him and show him which kind of kisses you like the most. Some men tend to be domineering when it comes to kissing—pushing their tongues into a woman's mouth without giving the woman the opportunity to return the compliment. Since women derive as much pleasure as men from tongue-exploring the inside of their partners' mouths, kissing should be share and share alike.

Now is also the time to tell him if his shaving habits irritate you. Not many men realize how much their stubble can burn a woman's skin. Since you don't want to finish up after every kissing bout with a reddened mouth and chin, you better suggest that he (a)shaves properly; or (b)grows himself a beard. Remind him that regular shaving is a courtesy that will affect not only your kissing, but oral sex, too.

The last thing you want to have scraping against your delicate vaginal tissues is a chin like Grade-3 sandpaper.

Your lover should kiss your lips, your face, your eyes, your ears, your neck. If you like him to bite your neck lightly during lovemaking, tell him—but remind him that visible lovebites are a no-no. You don't want to look like a teenage checkout girl the night after her first heavy date.

Kissing is one of the first sexual activities to suffer in a long-term sexual relationship. Over and over I hear the same complaint: "He never kisses me any more. All he does is make love to me, peck me on the cheek, and turn over."

But kissing is a wonderful expression of affection, as well as being arousing. A man who can kiss well can use his kisses to draw his partner toward him, both physically and emotionally; and he can also use kisses to increase her level of sexual arousal to a remarkably high pitch, even before he's touched her anyplace intimate.

Part of the problem of women not being able to reach orgasm in long-term sexual relationships is because their lovers haven't taken enough time and trouble to arouse them sufficiently *before* the act of intercourse. Most women report that if they indulge in ten minutes of unhurried kissing and caressing, this makes an immeasurable difference to their enjoyment of the intercourse that follows, and makes it nearly *three times* more likely that they will be able to reach a climax.

"I never know why Brad is in such a hurry," said twenty-nine-year-old Sylvia, from Austin, Texas. "We've got the whole evening. We've got the whole night. We've got the whole year. Yet he's in and out of me like a jumping jackrabbit."

Now your lover can concentrate on kissing your

shoulders (there are some very erotically-sensitive areas around the base of the neck); and then your breasts.

To be brutally honest, very few men have much of a clue when it comes to caressing a woman's breasts. The most common mishandling fault is to treat them as if they're two large car horn bulbs, and keep tooting them as if they expect them to go "beep beep!"

A few women enjoy having their breasts squeezed quite roughly during the most intense moments of lovemaking. But for most women, to have their breasts caressed sensitively and gently is sufficient to give them a whole variety of highly erotic feelings; and very occasionally even to bring them to orgasm.

Because of the highly-visual way in which they respond to sexual stimuli, men can be clumsy about your feelings when it comes to your breasts. Many big-breasted women have complained that their lovers treat their breasts "almost like they're not even part of me . . . as if they're some kind of toy stuck on the front of my chest for him to play with any way he likes." No matter how dazzled and aroused a man may be by the size of his partners' breasts, a little extra thought for her whole personality would take him a very long way. That doesn't mean he shouldn't say how much he adores her breasts or how much they turn him on. But it does mean that he should treat them gently and appreciatively and occasionally lift his gaze away from them and look her in the eye.

While most men are immediately aroused by very big breasts, they fail to realize that they can be a burden as well as a source of pride. This is Jackie, nineteen, a sales assistant in a department store in Toledo, Ohio: "My breasts started to develop when

I was twelve years old, and by the time I was fourteen I was 36C. Of course all the boys used to whistle at me, and men used to stare at me in the street, but believe me I hated it. I felt like some kind of animal in a zoo. I used to kneel down by the bed at night and pray to God that in the morning my breasts would be smaller. But of course they weren't. By the time I was sixteen I was 40DD, and that's what I am now.

"There are so many problems. I can never find any fashionable clothes that fit properly. Sometimes I have to buy two bikinis instead of one because the shop won't give me the top of one and the bottom of another. It's almost impossible to buy pretty bras. Most of them look like scaffolding. Even then the straps chafe because my breasts are so heavy. And even turning over in bed is a problem. I have to lift one breast over and then the other.

"About a year ago, I was seriously considering having a breast-reduction, and I probably would have done it if my parents could've afforded it. I'll definitely have it done one day, when I get older and my breasts start to sag. But my new boyfriend Donald is so tremendous and makes me feel so good about myself that I really don't mind at the moment. I know he likes my breasts being so big, they turn him on. But he doesn't react to them in the way that most of my high school dates used to react. Most of them would take me out, buy me a hamburger, and then expect to get straight into my blouse. Some of them didn't even bother about the hamburger. They treated me like a pair of walking tits with a girl who just happened to be attached to them.

"Donald was totally different. He asked me out, he took me to an alternative theater. He took me out for a Korean meal, which I'd never tried before. He asked me what I thought of the play. He asked me my politics. For the first time I felt that I was going out with a guy who was interested in my personality as well as my looks.

"He never made any secret of the fact that he likes my breasts. If he'd said something like 'Breasts? What breasts?' I never would have believed him anyway. But when he took me back to his apartment for the first time, he treated me like a complete woman all the time. We sat on the couch with a bottle of wine, and he spent a whole lot of time talking to me and kissing me. By the time he first caressed my breasts through my dress I was already turned on. I could feel that my panties were wet, and I really wanted him. But he didn't rush. He unbuttoned my dress and opened it and drew it down from my shoulders. He took a long look at me. I was wearing a black gauzy bra, just about the gauziest one that I was able to find in my size, and my nipples were standing out.

"Donald said, 'You're beautiful. You know that? You're perfect.' And it was that word "perfect" that I really loved him for. He didn't say 'Gee, what terrific knockers' (I've had that once or twice), and he didn't sit there with his mouth open, like some boys used to do.

"He gently touched my nipples through my bra, teasing them a little. Then he reached around and unfastened it; and that was another plus. He knew how to unfasten a bra. So many guys twist and fumble and just can't manage it, and you end up having to unfasten it yourself, which tends to take a whole lot of the fun and romance out of it."

Jackie was right. But it takes only a little simple skill to unfasten a bra, no matter how tight it might be. Almost all bras are fixed with flattish hooks-

and-eyes which defy an outward tug or a lustful twist, but which immediately come undone if the upper side of the backstrap is slid half-an-inch over the lower side. If the man in your life still hasn't mastered the art, you should show him how.

Jackie went on: "My bra came loose, my breasts bounced out of it. And do you know what he did? The very first thing he did? He kissed me. *Before* he even looked at my breasts. And then he cupped my breasts in his hands and circled his thumbs very softly and tantalizingly around and around my nipples. He kissed me again, and it was only then that he looked at my breasts and gently squeezed them. He kissed my nipples, one after the other, and then smiled at me and said, 'You're perfect.' Again, 'perfect.' That perfect word.

"He's a great lover. He never tries anything particularly spectacular. But he always takes his time. And he *does* pay a whole lot of attention to my breasts, without making them seem like they're more important than *I* am. One of my favorite things is to sit on top of him when we're making love, with his cock right up inside me as deep as it will go, and to swing my breasts over his face so that he can catch my nipples in his mouth. He sucks my nipples in deep and presses them right up against the roof of his mouth with his tongue, and I just adore that feeling."

Your lover should now caress your breasts and, while he's doing it, you should be showing him and telling him what excites you the most. Most women respond to a firm but gentle massaging of their breasts and a fingertip caressing their nipples. He can roll your nipples between finger and thumb, or gently twist them and tug them. Some women like to have their nipples pulled and twisted quite hard as they approach orgasm. If that's something that you enjoy, you should tell your lover, and give him some idea of how hard.

Make sure that your lover takes his time with your breasts. Too frequently, men give their lovers a few quick kisses on each nipple, and then promptly disappear lower down for more direct sexual activity. But they're making a serious mistake by being in such a hurry. Kissing and sucking and licking a woman's breasts is one of the best ways to prepare her for intercourse, and ultimately for orgasm. Most women will show some signs of vaginal lubrication after their breasts have been caressed, and as I mentioned before, some women are capable of reaching a climax through breast caresses alone.

Women with smaller breasts often complain that their lovers spend "almost no time at all" caressing them. Yet of course their breasts are just as erotically sensitive as their more generously-endowed sisters. Not only that, *all* the reports that I have received of climaxes being brought on by breast-stimulation alone have come from small-breasted women. Whether this might lead us to suppose that smaller breasts are even more susceptible to sexual stimulation than larger breasts—well, there's no scientific way of telling. But there's one thing we should know for sure, small-breasted women have an equal need for breast caresses as large-breasted women.

Sometimes, more so. For many small-breasted women are very self-conscious about their lack of size, and feel that they lack femininity and sex-appeal. Hardly surprising since many men make their response to large-breasted women so glaringly obvious. But if the lovers of small-breasted women not only told them that they were beautiful, but made it clear how sexy they thought they were by devoting much more time to caressing their breasts and stimulating their nipples, they would reap their rewards in heavenly sexual intercourse.

One of the best definitions I ever heard of the perfect breast was "a breast which can be completely contained in a lover's hand." So if you're small-breasted, take that as a classic compliment.

While we're talking about small breasts, it's worth mentioning breast enlargement. Personally, I'm against it. I've been asked about it scores of times by women who feel that they could revitalize their collapsing marriage or their burned-out affair "if only I had a larger, more shapely bosom."

My answer to that is that people make relationships, not breasts. And although I freely admit that there are thousands of women who have been delighted with their larger breasts, and have lived happily ever after . . . those women have almost invariably wanted the operation for the sake of personal vanity, *not* to rescue an ailing relationship.

Quite apart from why you may want it done, the surgical enlargement of the breasts is extremely expensive, almost always disappointing, and occasionally disfiguring or even dangerous.

So make the most of the beautiful breasts you've been given by God; and make sure that your lover appreciates them, too.

Of course there are such things on the market as "breast developers." These are plastic cups which you place over your breasts and then evacuate (that is, you pump the air out of them). Since nature abhors a vacuum, your breast is sucked into the cup to take the place of the evacuated air, thus making your breast swell bigger!

These "developers" would be terrific if you could walk around all the time with two plastic vacuum-cups on your breasts, but unfortunately your breasts return to their normal size when you take them off, and there is no evidence that they have any lasting effect. Some users say they feel nice, but that's about as far as it goes. Save your $50.

There's a "penis-developer" which works on the same principle—a transparent plastic tube into which a man inserts his penis. When he evacuates air from the tube, his penis swells to fill it. The result can be spectacular. Unfortunately, it's a question of "you can look, but you can't touch," because as soon as the air is let back in again, the penis returns to its regular size.

Perhaps the real reason that men buy "penis-developers" is given away by a small note in the catalog: "This product will also make an excellent masturbating aid as you can masturbate in a continually erect state and explode into a vacuum." Doesn't bode well for sex in space, does it?

Another mechanical aid to "breast-development" is a vibrator with a cup fixed to the end which is supposed to massage your breasts into new youthful firmness. Again, the consumer test report seems to be that it's mildly sexy to use, but has no noticeable effect on the firmness of your bustline. Save your $45.50.

As he continues his caresses of your breasts, your lover can suck your nipples, "drumming" them with the tip of his tongue; or gently bite them if you find it exciting to have them nipped. You can encourage him to massage your breasts with his erect penis, too. Although this form of foreplay is more visually stimulating than physically stimulating, it can help your lover to maintain or increase his hardness as he arouses you.

He can sit astride you and slide his penis into your cleavage, and massage your breasts against his erect shaft with his hands. Or he can massage your nipples with the head of his penis—a caress which will most likely be enhanced by the clear pre-ejaculatory lubricant which his penis is exuding. At this time you can join in the foreplay by bending your head forward and kissing and licking his cock.

Ellie, twenty-three, a short-order waitress from Butte, Montana, wrote me, "I'm quite large-breasted, i.e. I've been able to lift my breasts and suck my own nipples since I was about sixteen. I used to do it when I masturbated and it made it ten times more of a turn-on. Now when my boyfriend makes love to me I can take his cock and my own nipple into my mouth both at the same time, and that really gets him excited, rubbing and squeezing his cock around my nipple while I'm licking and lapping all around them."

Of course not every woman can manage to suck her own nipples, but your lover will find it very arousing if you lick his penis with a generous amount of saliva and then use his well-moistened glans to massage your breasts.

Gradually now, your lover can move down your body, kissing and stroking and caressing. He will be able to make your loveplay last longer (and of course, arouse you even more) if he bypasses your pussy for now and works his way down to your feet and your thighs. Very few men realize that a firm but gentle massaging of a woman's feet can give her some very pleasurable sensations, especially when it's accompanied by kisses and caresses of her back or thighs or those sensitive spots around her hip-bones.

Many women also find that if their lover is holding and caressing their feet, while at the same time stroking their hair or kissing their shoulders, that they experience a reassuring feeling of being small and protected, as if their lover is *encompassing* them. This is an assertion of virility that is almost ignored in most discussions about loveplay, but the overall way in which your lover behaves is in many ways just as important to your arousal as any specific caress.

While caressing you, your lover should be decisive, comprehensive, and considerate. That is, he should know what he wants to do to you, and do it without fumbling. He should arouse every part of you, not just your breasts and your vagina. And he should caress you in a way that isn't irritating or painful or awkward. At the same time, he should try to take his caresses to the limit—trying out anything and everything that takes his fancy.

If he *does* want to experiment, it's critically important that you don't react in a negative way. Not just during this Mutual Discovery Session, but at any time. There are few things more damaging to a man's self-confidence than being told that his sexual caresses are disgusting or unwanted.

If you don't happen to like what he does, then you can discuss it later, calmly and lightly, when all the sexual pressure is off. But don't try to put him off in the heat of the moment, or you'll almost certainly cause problems, and probably bring your afternoon of romantic self-discovery to an abrupt and unpleasant end.

"Jim always liked to bite my neck and scratch my back," said twenty-eight-year-old Velma, a sales assistant from San Diego. "I used to enjoy it *occasionally*, right at the very beginning of our relationship, when Jim was still married to his wife and there was a kind of danger about what we were doing. But after a while I got pretty tired of all those red marks on my neck and all those scratches on my back. When he started biting, I froze up, and pushed away from him, and then he got all angry and upset and started saying, 'What? What?'

and our lovemaking got really messed up. In the end, though, when we were walking on the beach one day, I plucked up the courage and told him that I loved him, but I simply didn't like being bitten and scratched. He said, 'Okay,' and that was the end of it. I think in any sexual relationship you have to make yourself very clear . . . but of course it's difficult to make yourself clear when you're right in the middle of making love. The tension's always running too high."

That was sensible advice. No matter how loving and understanding he may be, the fact is that when a man is sexually aroused, his natural aggressiveness is also aroused. As one sex therapist put it: "Equality of the sexes does not take away the urge of men to capture and conquer, or the need of women to feel possessed. Part of the role of a woman is to stimulate and provoke her lover into the passionate response she needs for her own fulfillment. A woman can, and should, play an active part in lovemaking, yet the male is the one who enters and the woman is the one who is entered, so that a certain primal element of 'male dominance' will still be present, however reciprocal loving becomes. The mixture of dominance, acceptance, and reciprocity in all this will depend on the individual natures of the lovers, and their sensitivity to one another's needs."

Some women enjoy a certain amount of rough or even painful loveplay. If this is something that you've always wanted to try, then now's the time to suggest it. But whatever you ask your lover to do, make sure that he understands the rules. The second you say, 'Honest Injun,' that's the second he has to stop.

"When I married Mack, he was thirty-nine and I was only nineteen," said twenty-four-year-old

Gayle, from Charleston, South Carolina. "We used to play a kind of a game together. If ever we went out and I misbehaved myself, like making a fool of myself in company, or flirting with the waiters in a restaurant, Mack would take me home afterwards, and he'd spank me. I actually used to like it, it used to turn me on. At one time it used to turn me on so much that I used to misbehave on purpose just to make sure that he'd do it.

"I remember one of the best times. We'd been over to his sister's house for dinner, and I'd spent the whole evening batting my eyelashes at his sister's husband Rex. I knew that Mack was getting jealous and riled, so I did it even more; and even put my hand on Rex's knee under the table and blew in his ear and stuff like that. When we got home, Mack totally exploded. He told me to come into the bedroom, lift up my skirt and lie down over his knee.

"I guess I was being extra-disobedient that evening because I wouldn't. I tried to make a run for the door, but he caught me, and he twisted my arm, and he marched me back into the bedroom. He sat down on the bed, forced me down over his knees and pulled up my skirt at the back. I was wearing a black garter belt and black stockings and black panties, too. But I always wore my panties *under* my garter belt so he couldn't pull them down, not without taking my stockings off. But he tugged my panties right up between the cheeks of my bottom so that I was as good as bare.

"Then he took that smooth wooden hairbrush he always used, and he smacked me with it. I yelped out loud because he'd never hit me as hard as that before. Then he smacked me again, and again.

"That hairbrush really stung. But at the same time it made the cheeks of my bottom feel real hot and tingly. And the more he did it, the hotter and tinglier I got, and the feeling seemed to spread right down from my bottom and between my legs. He stopped spanking me, and said, 'That's enough.' But I said, 'More, Mack, more,' which was about all that I could manage to say because I was so breathless.

"He spanked me again, and again, and again. My bottom felt like it was glowing. I managed to wrestle one arm free, and I reached down into my panties. They were soaking. They were so wet that they'd left a damp patch on Mack's pants, too. I flicked myself with my finger, which is all that I could do with my hand wedged in like that, but Mack kept on spanking me, and that hot, hot glow just swelled right over me, and before I knew what was happening I was clinging on to Mack's legs, and I was shaking like a leaf. It seemed like one orgasm after another, it didn't seem to stop.

"He doesn't spank me any more. Times have changed, and I guess I've grown up. But I still feel like it once in a blue moon, when I'm feeling frisky and naughty, and I think it's time for Mack to remind me what's what."

Incidentally, the mild sadism in Gayle's relationship wasn't exclusively one-way. This was her own special sexual technique which she described to me with some relish.

"I used to lie back on the bed and coax Mack into sitting on top of me, and I'd let him rub my breasts with his cock. Then I'd take hold of his cock and lick it a while, running my tongue all the way down to his balls. He knew what was coming: it used to make him shudder. All of a sudden I'd take hold of one of his balls, and I'd cram it into my mouth. If he tried to get away I'd give it a little bite. Then I used to rub his cock up and down, real slow, as slow as I wanted to, because if he tried to argue I'd give his balls another bite. I mean, not really hard, but hard enough to stop him in his tracks.

"I used to keep on rubbing him until he was just about to climax. I could tell because his balls used to tighten up. It was fantastic because I could feel every single spurt, and I used to lick his balls with my tongue while he was doing it, and that used to drive him mad. Sometimes I used to squeeze the top of his foreskin together when he came so that none of his sperm spurted out. Then, when he was finished, I used to roll his foreskin down, and all this warm white sperm would come pouring down his cock like a melting candle, all over his balls and all over my lips, and I'd lick him and suck him until he was dry. There was always an extra when I did that: some of the sperm had stayed in his cock, so I could take his cock into my mouth and give it a deep suck and drink down the last mouthful that he had left."

Gayle's relationship became less sado-masochistic after her husband suffered a lengthy illness, but she confessed that she still hankered after "a little bit of spanking and a little bit of scratching."

Regrettably, the aggression that accompanies sex can sometimes get out of hand. One woman reported that her husband regularly punched her ribs when he was climaxing, and I have heard of many cases in which a wife or girlfriend has been bruised or lacerated or hurt quite badly. These cases are very rarely reported because women are frightened of their lovers' anger, and also because to some extent—though not to the *whole* extent—they were willing partners to what happened and feel partly to blame.

But as I have said time and time again, a limited

degree of sadistic or masochistic behavior can add an enormous amount of spice and variety to a sexual relationship. But causing physical injury or mental distress are absolute, one hundred percent no-nos.

Whatever happens in a sexual relationship, your body is yours, and you always have the unconditional right to say "no."

What you will be saying "yes" to, though, is your lover's caresses of those responsive areas at the back of your calves, behind your knees, and up the inside of your thighs.

One of the most stimulating caresses of the thighs is a proper massage with massage-oil. Most drugstores these days sell some kind of suitable oil for massage, although you might care to kill two birds with one stone and use The Body Shop's cellulite massage-oil, which (besides being pleasantly perfumed and very suitable for erotic massage) has the added advantage of helping to slim down your thighs.

Your lover should use slow, strong, sensual movements—first massaging the front of your thighs, smoothing them upward away from the knees, then gradually moving his hands around to the outer side of your thighs, and upward, too.

He should bring the massage to a finish by massaging the backs of your thighs, higher and higher with each stroke, until his fingertips are just touching and very gently tugging at the outer lips of your vagina.

Even now—or perhaps *especially* now—both of you should remember not to hurry. Take things easy, savor every single moment, every single feeling.

You're ready now for the next stage of your

Mutual Discovery Session, which will open your body to your lover and at the same time open the doors to a love-life in which you will be enjoying varied and exciting lovemaking six days a week.

6

Open Wide: A Girl's Guide To Unashamed Sex

"I was always brought up to be modest. In our house we never walked around naked. I don't think I ever saw my mother without any clothes on. She always locked the bathroom door and never appeared without a robe. I found the idea of being naked with a boy was nerve-wracking enough. But the idea of opening up my legs and letting him look at me . . . well, it was out of the question."

That was Frannie, twenty-one, from Tarrytown, New York, who originally wrote to me about what she supposed was her "frigidity." In fact, she had a very strong sex drive. Her only problem was that she lacked sexual knowledge and technique; and without that knowledge and technique, she naturally lacked confidence.

She was embarrassed about showing herself, not just because she'd never shown herself to *anybody* before—not her husband or the two boyfriends with whom she'd slept before meeting him—but because she was concerned that her husband would think her a whore.

But no sexual relationship can be widened or improved unless you're both familiar with each other's sexual organs and frequently enjoy the sight, the feel, the taste, and the aroma of them. *Aroma?* I can hear some of you ask, nervously. Well, yes, for sure. Your vulva odor, the so-called *cassolette*, contains powerful chemicals that can arouse in men a tremendously strong sexual response.

Of course you should always keep yourself clean. But immediately prior to making love, you should never wash away all of those natural chemicals with perfumed soap or vaginal douches. You may think that you're making your private parts smell as sweet as a rose, but in fact you're not doing yourself any favors at all. Men are naturally and irresistibly attracted to the smell of your vulva; and as part of sexual foreplay, bodily kisses lead steadily and inexorably toward your genital area.

If you've been brought up to regard nudity as embarrassing and your sexual parts as something you'd rather not discuss, let alone stare at—let alone allow your *lover* to stare at—then of course it's not your fault. But if you want to take that Great Leap Forward in your sex life, then you're going to have to grit your teeth and open yourself up, regardless.

Remember what I said before about your vulva. It's yours, it's individual, but it's beautiful—and in your lover's eyes it's absolutely the most entrancing sight in the entire universe. Before your Mutual Discovery Session, you should have taken the opportunity to look through as many men's magazines as possible, just to get yourself used to the sight of women with their legs open, showing off their vulvas, and to the variety of different vulvas there are.

You may disapprove of women opening up their legs for magazines. But whatever your objections, *you*, unlike them, won't be exposing yourself in public. You'll be exposing yourself only for your lover, to show how much you adore him, to show how close you want to be to him. And apart from that, you'll be making a commitment to a far more exciting sex life.

When I talk about "exposing yourself", I don't just mean walking in and out of the bathroom with nothing on, or allowing him a quick flash when you're wearing no panties. I'm talking about lying back and opening your legs for him as wide as you can, and allowing him to look, and to touch, and to explore . . . the same way that you explored him.

If you haven't shown yourself off much to your lover before—not in so detailed and intimate a manner—then you're going to need to relax. That's part of the reason I suggested a thigh-massage as his foreplay approached your pussy. You should breathe gently, let yourself go, and tell yourself that he loves you, and that he's going to love you even more for sharing yourself with him so openly.

The question of pubic shaving comes up pretty frequently these days. Since swimsuits and leotards cut high on the hip are the current fashion, almost all women at least trim their pubic hair, and an increasingly large number shave it off altogether, or even have it permanently removed by electrolysis. Of course it's up to the taste of the individual. I've talked to some men who were furious when their wives and girlfriends shaved themselves; but not very many, and most of those were older men with rather rigid ideas about sexual display.

But most men are strongly aroused by the sight of a woman's vulva shaved completely bare. Men's magazines are showing more and more girls without pubic hair, and there are several magazines which devote themselves completely to pubic shaving— *Shaven Girls* and *Shaven Ravers* in Britain, the less-than-subtly titled *New Cunts* in Scandinavia, and *Rasierte* in Germany, which describes itself as "the new white-hot magazine with even more photos than you've ever seen before of depilated gorgeous girls who have shaved off all unwanted hair and who lay their treasures before you unhidden and unashamed."

Georgie, a twenty-six-year-old advertising executive from Chicago, said, "My mother was a very feminine and elegant woman. She groomed herself like a queen. She always waxed her legs and shaved off her pubic hair, and so as I grew up it was quite natural for me to do the same. She taught me how to do it properly—how to use plenty of soap and a fresh razor, and rub a little lotion on afterwards to cool any razor-burn, and that's what I did. I always felt it was much more hygienic and aesthetic, and when I saw girls in the changing-rooms who didn't do it I always felt that they were pretty scruffy and ungroomed, the same as if they hadn't shaved their underarms or plucked their eyebrows.

"I guess the first time I was conscious that not every girl did it was when I first slept with my boyfriend. We were lying on the couch getting into some pretty heavy kissing and fondling, and he slipped his hand into my panties. He said, 'Wow,' would you believe? He actually said, 'wow.' He really couldn't get over it. In fact he was so turned on that he ejaculated as soon as his cock touched my cunt. He didn't even get it in!

"I guess it was a good thing that it was my first time, and that I didn't really understand what had happened. We made love properly about an hour later, and even though it wasn't earth-shattering it was pretty damned nice. He adored my cunt, absolutely adored it. I mean, he kept *saying* so, he was so turned on. And he used to give me oral sex at least once or twice a night. I didn't realize that other girls didn't get it even half as often as I did. I never had any problem with orgasms!"

Many other women have discovered that clean-shaving their vulvas has increased their lovers' interest in oral sex. There are two plus factors involved: one is that men are strongly stimulated by the sight of your sexual organs as they become aroused. Without pubic hair, they can see absolutely everything. The other is that kissing a depilated vulva is very much more pleasant than kissing a hairy one. And as a woman becomes sexually aroused, her hairless lips become much more slippery with vaginal juice than they would if they were unshaved.

One or two women were worried that their lovers' principal interest in having them shave off their pubic hair was to see them looking like little girls. "I began to wonder if he was interested in child sex or something," remarked Nina, a twenty-eight-year-old homemaker from Los Angeles. But there is absolutely no evidence to justify that anxiety. Quite the opposite, in fact: the stimulus for most men seems to be that a fully-matured, full-breasted woman should be so openly displaying her vaginal lips.

Not only does it indicate to a man that the woman in his life is eager to show herself off to him, it shows that she is enthusiastic about their sex life and is prepared to do something special to turn him on. If you like, it's a visible sexual commitment.

Here's Rita, a thirty-three-year-old employment-agency manager from Dayton, Ohio: "I'll have been married to Barry for twelve years this Thanksgiving. We're both ambitious, both career-minded. Barry runs his own computer business and he's been expanding all over the Midwest. We always got along together, we always understood each other. We always gave each other space.

"But about a year-and-a-half ago, I suddenly woke up one morning, and I couldn't remember the last time we'd made love. We hadn't been arguing or anything, everything was running along real smooth. But then I thought, *too smooth*, you know? We got up, breakfasted together, read our respective newspapers, came back, had dinner together, watched a little television, went to bed. Sometimes we went to the theater or out for dinner. What a charming couple! But it was like something had gone, and what had gone was, we didn't bother to make love any more.

"I walked out of the bathroom naked that morning. Well, I walk out of the bathroom naked *every* morning. But that morning I realized that Barry didn't even take his eyes away from the breakfast show to look at me. Didn't even blink. I was tempted to say something, but I know Barry. He doesn't like to talk about personal stuff very much. So I kept my thoughts to myself.

"But at work that day, I kept thinking about it, and in the end I called one of my best friends, Joan, and we had lunch together. I told her what was wrong and she was very sympathetic. She said the same kind of thing had happened to her when she was first married. Their sex life had just dwindled away to nothing at all . . . not because they hated each other or anything like that. It was just because they'd gotten out of the habit. Unlike me, she'd complained about it, and she and her husband had terrible arguments. She said that he was a lousy lover, but he said that she'd never shown any interest in sex so why should he bother?

"Anyway, that stung her because she *adored* sex and had always thought that she was pretty damn sexy. So she read all the magazine articles and books she could read about what makes a woman sexually attractive, but all the women's magazines told her was to be flirty, and well-dressed, and what perfumes to use, and how to invite a man home for a sexy dinner-for-two. She reckoned that she knew all of that already, so instead she started looking at men's magazines to see what men really thought was sexy.

"She took four or five men's magazines to the office and handed them around to the men who worked there and told them to vote on what they thought was the sexiest picture. Four out of five of them voted for a blonde girl in stockings and a garter belt. She wasn't particularly busty, and she wasn't even particularly pretty, but she did have a completely shaved vagina.

"She said that none of the men would admit that was why they liked her. They all said 'I prefer blondes,' or 'she looks more intelligent.' But Joan wasn't fooled. That weekend she had her hair highlighted, she shaved off her pubic hair, and she bought herself red stockings and a red garter-belt. I said, 'Wasn't that pandering to the worst in your husband? I mean—wasn't that like admitting that you *weren't* very sexy, after all?'

"But her opinion was that if a relationship is breaking up, and you want to save it, then it doesn't really matter whose fault it is. What really matters is that whichever one of you has the *power* to save it should do whatever they can. 'I love him,' she said. 'Why should I worry about my pride?'

"And as it turned out, her husband really sat up and took notice. She didn't make any pretense about what she was doing. She gave it to him straight, like: 'I love you and I want to keep you and I'm going to turn you on whether you want me to or not.' And he responded, and they lived happily ever after, pretty much. At least they started having a regular sex life again.

"So I took a leaf out of Joan's book. I called the office and told them I wasn't too well. Then I went shopping. I bought myself some black stockings, a garter-belt, two little lacy thongs, and a new razor. Then I went home and ran myself a deep bath full of Chanel No. 5 bath gel. Before I got in, I stood in front of the mirror in the dressing-room and snipped off most of my pubic hair with nail-scissors. Then I got into the tub and I wallowed in it for almost three-quarters of an hour. I soaped myself between my legs and started to shave myself. I don't know why, but it turned me on, and frightened me a little, too. I got quite breathless. You have to be real careful shaving around your vaginal lips, but if you take your time it's fine. I took everything off so that it was totally smooth.

"How did I react? Well, without hair, I thought my vagina looked surprisingly neat and clean. It didn't look like a child's vagina at all; the mound was too pronounced, and my vaginal lips were exposed. After I was dry, I sat down on the bathroom rug with a mirror and opened my lips up with my fingers and looked at myself. You don't realize that your vagina is such a perfect arch-like shape. For the first time ever I actually thought that my vagina was beautiful. I felt more womanly; but I felt pretty damn daring, too. I was so turned on by what I was doing that the inside of my vagina was shining wet.

"I was quite tempted to masturbate then, for the first time in about seven years, and I did rub and caress myself a little. My vaginal lips started to swell and to look all flushed. Before I shaved off my pubic hair I never realized that happened. You don't realize that when you make love your sexual organs are responding just as noticeably as your husband's.

"I was waiting in the kitchen for Barry when he came home. My hair was brushed, I was sprayed with Chanel, and I was naked except for my black stockings and my black garter belt and a pair of black shiny high-heels. He came into the kitchen still wearing his coat and he stared at me like somebody had hit him with a baseball bat.

"I was terrified for a moment that he wasn't going to like it. But he came right up to me and looked me up and down and said, 'I must be dreaming! The *Playboy* center-spread just walked into my life.' He didn't ask me why, or what I was doing. It was just like a light-switch had clicked in his head and he'd noticed me again . . . noticed that I was sexy, and that I turned him on.

"We didn't even make the bedroom. I lay on the living-room rug and I lifted up both legs as high and as wide as I could. He threw off his coat and managed to wrestle his pants down, but he couldn't wait any longer. His cock was sticking up big and hard and dark, dark red. I took hold of it and it felt like a hot tree-trunk. Then I guided it down between my legs, and for the first time I could see the way my vagina parted so that his big cock-head could slide right inside me. I could see the way my lips clung to the shaft of his cock as he went in and out. I could *feel* more, too. I could feel his pubic hair brushing and tickling me, I could feel the wetness between us, I could feel his balls swaying against me. It was like I'd always been making love with gloves on, and now I'd taken them off.

"When he came, he lifted himself halfway out of me, and I could see his sperm welling up all around his cock, bubbling like hot white lava. Then he slowly took his cock out, still dripping a few last drips on to my bare vagina, and I could watch his sperm pouring slowly down between the cheeks of my bottom.

"It was so stunning because I could see it all, as well as feel it, and that was a totally new experience. You don't have to ask; our sex life is very much better. As a matter of fact there are times when I have to ask Barry to give me some peace. His favorite way of falling asleep these days is with his head against my shoulder and his hand between my legs."

Of course, shaving off your pubic hair doesn't automatically guarantee you a rejuvenated sex life. You may think, for example, that your lover isn't too keen on it, in which case you might do better to ask (playfully) if he'd like it. But, as we've seen, most men find it strongly arousing, largely because it's immediate and irrefutable evidence that you're just as keen on sex as they are . . . if not more so.

While we're on the subject, you may like to suggest to your lover that *he* shave his pubic hair off, too. While many women like very hairy men, there are an increasingly number who would like their partners at least to trim their straggling pubes, especially those whom enjoy oral sex.

Wanda, twenty-seven, a fabric designer from Minneapolis, said, "I said to John one night, 'I'm going to shave your cock,' and I did, and it was amazing. You may like giving a man head, but when you've licked the totally bare penis and balls of a grown man with a huge erection, you've never experienced anything. You can suck it and kiss it all over, balls and everything. The skin is so silky, it's beautiful, and you don't get all that fur in your mouth. It doesn't make your lover less of a man. Personally, I think it makes him *more* of a man. It makes his cock look instantly about two inches longer, for sure. First of all, John was worried about what the other guys would say when he went into the showers after squash, but they didn't say anything, and so he said 'what the hell.' These days he stands in the showers and openly shaves his cock as well as his chin.''

Whether you have decided to shave yourself or not, you should now be lying on your bed with your thighs wide apart so that both you and your lover can explore your vulva. You will have noticed, incidentally, that some women tend to call their genitalia their "vagina" while some use the word "vulva." In fact, "vulva" is a composite term for all of your *external* sexual parts, the parts outside of your body. The vagina is the actual tube which ensheaths the penis during intercourse.

It's useful to have a mirror at this point of the Mutual Discovery Session so that you can watch while your lover explores you. A hand-mirror is usually the best because you can control it yourself, and it's not too obtrusive. You should also make sure that you are lying in a position in which your vulva is very well lit.

Again . . . I know that's it not easy for some women to open themselves up so intimately to their husbands or lovers. But opening yourself up both physically and emotionally is the key to exciting lovemaking. The reason why so many relationships gradually grind down is because one or both partners is always holding something back—either for fear of committing themselves too deeply, or because they have needs and desires which they believe their partner will find disgusting or ridiculous.

You want to have sex six days a week—more if possible. You want to have far more stimulating sex. Getting to know your partner and allowing your partner to know you is the only way in which you will be able to achieve it. This a time for daring to say what you think. This is a time for daring to admit what you need. This is a time for doing things that you only fantasized about.

You shouldn't look on this close-up inspection of your vulva as a one-off, either—"you've seen it all once, don't tell me you want *another* look?" Your lover will want to look at you and play with you again and again . . . in fact, he'll never grow tired of it, and nor should you.

Miriam, a thirty-one-year-old magazine editor from New York, said, "There's nothing I find more pleasurable than lying on the bed in the evening after work, reading a book or watching television and sharing a bottle of wine, while Michael gently fingers my cunt. He can do it for hours, as far as I'm concerned. Sometimes I could almost fall asleep, it's so delightful. Other times, it leads us gradually up to lovemaking."

Your sexual parts are yours, and there will obviously be times when you *don't* want to be touched or fondled. Then you have the inalienable right to say "hands to yourself, pal," and expect to be obeyed. Just like *you* wouldn't continue chomping on his penis when he had obviously had enough, would you? (Although I haven't yet met the man who's ever had enough.)

With your thighs wide apart, the outer lips of your vulva will have opened, revealing the thin pale inner lips, which are usually closed to protect the opening to the vagina. Since you are probably sexually aroused by now, and you have opened your legs very wide, the inner lips will probably be wholly or partially open too, revealing your vagina.

If they're not, your lover should gently part them so that he can see inside. At the top, where the lips join together in a pointed arch, he'll see the center of your sexual pleasure, your clitoris—the organ that in 1960s free-love slang was called the "love-button."

There used to be a myth among sexually-ignorant men that a woman's clitoris was like a secret "switch." They had only to touch it, and a woman would turn instantly into a panting nymphomaniac. Being better-educated, your lover will know that gentle, persistent stroking or flicking of the clitoris is required to arouse you . . . sometimes, depending on your mood and your surroundings, for some considerable time. Men who lack staying-power of either finger or tongue are advised to rush off at once and do some strenuous exercises.

The "button" of the clitoris is in fact only the tip of the iceberg. It is no more than the equivalent of the glans (or head) of your lover's penis. Buried beneath the "button" is a shaft of two rods of tissue, closely linked, known as the *corpora cavernosa*. Your lover will be able to feel this shaft beneath your skin just above the glans.

Just like the corpora cavernosa in your lover's penis, these tissues can become swollen with blood when you're sexually excited, making your clitoris bigger—but you can't, of course, have an erection.

Incidentally, if your lover inserts his finger into your vagina and, with a "wagging" motion, puts rhythmic pressure on the underside of your clitoris through your vaginal wall, he will usually give you an extremely pleasurable and stimulating sensation. He might even be able to bring you to a climax. This technique of internal clitoral stimulation has been used since women first developed clitorises to be stimulated, but it was triumphantly rediscovered some years ago and called the "G-Spot." If you want to know where your "G-Spot" is, that's it.

Clitorises vary in size and shape just as much as

penises. The glans can vary from one-eighth of an inch to nearly half-an-inch in diameter, and the buried shaft can be long and thin or short and fat, or anything in between. Pornographic fiction frequently talks about women with "prominent clitorises," but the size or shape of your clitoris doesn't make the slightest difference to your sexual responsiveness.

There are several African tribes whose young girls spend hours massaging their labia and their clitorises for the specific purpose of increasing their sexual pleasure. The result of this massage is that by the time they reach puberty, their vulvas and clitorises are considerably enlarged. This may make them more attractive to their mates, but there is no evidence at all that they have a better time in bed, or in the hammock, or wherever, than women with normal sized clitorises.

What *does* make a difference is the number of tiny pressure-sensitive corpuscles in your clitoris. Some women have an abundance of them, others have fewer, although nobody knows why, and regrettably there is nothing that anybody can do to increase clitorial sensitivity, except to increase the stimulus applied to it.

Show and tell your lover how you like your clitoris to be touched. Even the world's greatest lover doesn't know what you feel like inside when your clitoris is stimulated. He doesn't know whether you like your clitoris rubbed with one finger or two; whether you like it rapidly flicked with the side of his finger; whether you like his touch to be gentle or firm.

Some women like to have their clitorises massaged quite forcefully around and around; others prefer to have the lightest of butterfly-flicks. If you want your lover to give you exactly what you want, then it's up to you to show him.

The clitorial shaft is attached to a muscle which is the equivalent of the muscle in your lover's body which rhythmically contracts during his climax and shoots semen out through his penis. This muscle divides into two, passing either side of the vagina. When you have an orgasm, it contracts rhythmically and causes regular contractions of the outer part of your vagina.

Although there are similarities between the penis and the clitoris, they don't respond in anything like the same way when they're sexually stimulated. Clitoral response, for instance, is nothing as immediate as the erection of the penis; your clitoris doesn't begin to enlarge until it has been well-stimulated—long after your vagina has become lubricated.

Your clitoris doesn't grow in size in the same proportion as your lover's penis, although every woman's clitoris does grow large enough to bring it into contact with the folds of skin around it, which helps to increase stimulation of the nerve-endings.

Direct stimulation of the glans of the clitoris is not necessarily essential to bring you to orgasm. In any case, your clitoris almost always withdraws out of sight and out of direct touch as orgasm approaches, and the stimulation which eventually brings on orgasm is usually that of the muscles on either side of the vaginal lips being rhythmically tugged by your lover's penis, or fingers, or tongue.

However, if your lover is stimulating your clitoris with his finger when it withdraws, remind him to keep on going, regardless. You'll know for yourself how frustrating it can be if he suddenly stops caressing you there, just because it's disappeared, and he mistakenly thinks that you've "gone off the boil."

Apart from being regarded by some men as an instant turn-on switch, there are many other fallacies surrounding the clitoris. Until Masters & Johnson undertook their laboratory studies of orgasm, it was widely held that there are two types of orgasm—the clitoral, which was exciting but superficial, and the vaginal, which was deeper and more satisfying.

This fallacy was largely rooted in old-fashioned prejudices against masturbation and anything other than good honest married intercourse. But Masters & Johnson showed that it was completely false. There is only one type of orgasm, although the feelings you experience during orgasm may vary widely because of how you're being stimulated, who you're being stimulated by, where, and why.

During orgasm, the outer part of the vagina contracts in strong spasm, gripping your lover's penis tightly; and then breaks into a series of rhythmic contractions. As it contracts, it tugs even more strongly on the clitoral shaft and gives you all of those overwhelming feelings that you associate with orgasm.

After orgasm, however, your clitoris will return very quickly to its normal size and its normal exposed position above the vagina. The only time when it remains engorged with blood is when you've been aroused to fever pitch and then failed to reach a climax. This engorgement can last for hours afterwards, giving you a terrible feeling of frustration.

Time after time, I have to answer disappointed and frustrated lovers who can't understand why they rarely (if ever) reach simultaneous orgasm. After all, it happens in the movies, doesn't it? Fireworks, waterfalls, crashing waves.

But I always have to answer that simultaneous orgasm during intercourse happens, for most people, comparatively rarely—it at all. It can be done if your lover uses particular techniques, the least complicated of which is for him to penetrate you from behind and to reach around and stimulate your clitoris and your vaginal lips during intercourse. He may also have to stop thrusting now and then in order to hold back his own climax. When he becomes more skillful, he may be able to take himself right to the brink of his own climax, and then keep his penis quite still, sheathed deeply inside you, so that when *you* come, the orgasmic contractions of your vagina are sufficient to bring him off, too.

You won't want to use this technique all the time, however—especially when you start to increase your lovemaking to six days a week (and then some). So there will inevitably be times when *he* climaxes and you don't quite manage it. Despite everything they say about "nice guys finishing last," it isn't always possible for a man to hold back his ejaculation for as long as he would like. It's like the man who was making love to his girlfriend on the railroad tracks. After a speeding express train had screeched to a last-minute halt to avoid hitting them, he said to the irate engineer, "Sorry, but I was coming, and she was coming, and you was coming. But you was the only one who had brakes." Not only that, but if a man holds his climax back for too long, he can seriously spoil the spontaneity and pleasure of his lovemaking. And the last thing you want to do is put him off!

The answer then is for you to make it obvious to him after intercourse has finished that you need still more stimulation to satisfy you.

This isn't always as easy as it sounds, especially if you're tired or if you've been drinking. Most men abruptly lose interest in sex as soon as they ejaculate, and to be brutally truthful it takes an especially considerate man to continue stimulating you to orgasm after he has reached his own climax.

Here's Rosanna, from Austin, Texas, a thirty-one-year-old homemaker: "Bill was never a bad lover. He always loved me; he still loves me today. He's sexy, too. He works outdoors and he's got this lovely lean muscular body, not a spare ounce anywhere. But he hardly ever satisfied me in bed. He'd work me up good, kissing my lips, kissing my breasts, holding and caressing me. But once he'd gotten himself inside of me, he was always just a tad too quick. I'd be just about to see stars, and suddenly he'd shout out, and that'd be the end of it. After that, he'd kiss me a while and tell me he loved me. But he wouldn't try to help me come. I guess he thought he *had* made me come, or at least that I didn't need to. I mean, what do you say to this man who's all panting and sweaty and proud— that he didn't do nothing for you? You just can't. Next thing I knew, he'd've fell asleep, and I was left wondering whether it'd be wrong for me to masturbate. I didn't used to at first, because I thought there was definitely something wrong if a married woman had to masturbate. But then I talked to one of my very best friends and *she* said that she never had any difficulty in coming to a climax with her husband, but she still masturbated now and then because she felt like it. She said, 'You're not going to wear it away.' But she also said that I should tell Bill what was wrong. I tried, believe me. I kept trying to bring the subject around to our lovemaking. But somehow I couldn't find the words. Me and Bill'd been married for too long. What was he going to say? 'We've been married for six years and *now* you tell me you're not satisfied?' "

My advice to Rosanna was to take matters into

her own hands, and to use self-stimulatory lovemaking techniques which would increase the chances of her reaching a climax before or during intercourse; and also to coax Bill into continuing his sexual stimulation if she failed to climax before he did.

As we have seen, many sex partners find lovemaking easy but discussion difficult. You can overcome this reticence by *showing* your lover what you need, without a word. Somehow a gently-guiding hand is less upsetting than even the most diplomatic suggestion.

I suggested she take a little longer preparing herself for bed. Pay some extra-special attention to her hair, her nails, her general grooming. Pay some extra-special attention to herself. Buy some new perfume, and some new bath-oil, and always *relax* before she went to bed.

As far as possible, I suggested she try to put her anxieties and frustrations about her lovemaking in the back of her mind. Try not to be panicky about it, or expect too much. Then, after her bath, she should spend a few minutes massaging her vulva and clitoris with a little baby oil, and thinking of all her favorite erotic fantasies.

When she was making love, I recommended that she used every possible technique to heighten her own stimulation. When Bill was kissing her, she should wrap her thighs around his leg and use rhythmic muscular squeezing to put pressure on her clitoral area. As he began to kiss her breasts, she should guide one of his hands downward and show him (without necessarily saying anything) how she best liked her clitoris to be stimulated.

Rushing into penetration too quickly is one of the commonest but one of the worst male faults in sexual technique. If only more men held off for as long as they possibly could before entering the woman in their lives, they (and those women) would be sexually more satisfied to the *nth* degree.

Of course it's hard to resist. Of course nature is urging both of you to start intercourse as soon as possible and multiply the human race. But it's your self-indulgent resistance to that urge that makes human sex so highly erotic. During so-called "foreplay," you and your lover can achieve startling new heights of sexual pleasure, and the longer you resist intercourse, the longer that pleasure is going to last.

Rosanna managed to follow my recommendations and extend her foreplay with Bill to lengths (and heights) that she had never dreamed of. Every time he tried to climb on top of her and penetrate her, she found a way of stalling him—but also of stimulating herself.

"The first time he got on top of me, I took hold of his hard-on, and instead of guiding it up inside me, I pressed it up against my clitoris, and massaged it around and around, just the way I like to massage myself. With my other hand, I held Bill's balls and softly kind of juggled them. He didn't raise no objection, in fact he was breathing real hard, and he kept leaning down and kissing me, and kissing my nipples, too.

"I reached down with both hands, and stretched open the hole in the end of his hard-on with my two thumbs. His hard-on was deep purple, and all of this clear juice came welling up from the hole. I pressed my clitoris up against him, so that it kind of fitted into the groove in his hard-on, and then I massaged it around and around a whole lot more, real slow.

"He wanted to push himself into me then, but I wriggled myself down between his legs, until I was far enough down to kiss his hard-on. I'd never done it before. Well, I think once I gave it a quick peck, when I was drunk, after my brother's 21st birthday. I was real nervous. I thought Bill might not take it so good. But he didn't say nothing, he just looked down at me, and there was this dreamy look on his face, so I knew that he liked it.

"I licked all around his hard-on with my tongue right out, licking it like it was a Sno-cone. Then when it was all shiny with spit I took it right in my mouth, so far that I practically choked, but for some reason I didn't mind the choking because this was my husband's hard-on, right inside my mouth. I was actually sucking and licking a man's hard-on, and I could do it for as long as I liked.

"With one hand I was holding his hard-on. With the other hand I was slowly massaging my clitoris, tugging it and pulling it and giving myself all those real deep feelings.

"I pushed Bill gently with one hand to show him that I wanted him to roll over on to his back. He wasn't used to lying on his back when we made love, but he wasn't used to *any* of this kind of treatment, and he didn't argue none. Then, I climbed on top of him and held open my vagina with both hands, and Bill pushed his hard-on right up inside me. Blonde hair tangling with black hair so that you couldn't see where one ended and the other began.

"I liked the feeling, sitting on top of him. It made lovemaking seem so much lighter, so much sexier. And his hard-on went so far up inside me. If I sat right back and pushed myself down, he touched my womb. I could sit there and stir myself around and his hard-on was massaging my womb like some kind of cement-mixer right inside me. I could feel his balls against my bottom, too, and I really liked the feeling of that. But the best thing was that I could lean forward, and when I leaned forward, and rode up and down on him, I could press my clitoris in just the right way. For the first time ever, *I* was the one in control.

"We fucked like crazy that night. And that was the first time ever that I had a climax before Bill. I didn't know what was happening at first. All I could feel was that huge hard-on plunging up inside me. Then I felt like the whole sky had cracked open. Bill said I was screaming out loud, but I don't recall doing that. Afterwards we lay tight together and we didn't speak. But I felt so good. I felt like I'd been swimming all of my life and at last I'd been washed up on the beach."

Rosanna's more positive sexual techniques also helped her when she was unable to reach orgasm before Bill had ejaculated.

She refused to let anxiety and frustration affect her lovemaking—even if she was fairly sure that Bill would come first. Then, when he *had* come, she would adopt one or more of the following techniques:

1) She would take hold of his hand and draw it down between her legs, guiding his fingertips on to her clitoris.

2) She would get up and kneel beside him on the bed, her head facing toward the foot of the bed, her calf pressed against his side, bend forward, and take his softening penis into her mouth, gently sucking the last of his semen, and swirling his penis around with her tongue. (I emphasize *gently*, because your lover's penis can be very sensitive immediately after ejaculation.)

Incidentally, many women only seem to consider oral sex when their lovers are mightily erect. But sucking a soft penis can be a great pleasure for both of you . . . and it's an extremely effective way of making even the sulkiest of penises quickly stiffen.

3) Or she would sit astride him, and offer her vulva to his ministering tongue.

She said: "I'll never forget the first time I sat on him like that. I think he was expecting to watch television for a while and then go to sleep. But I climbed up on to him and sat astride his face with my knees in the pillow.

"Of course the bedside lamp was shining bright . . . it always is. I've never much liked to make love in the dark. Bill looked up, and I looked down at him. My vagina was set and the lips were all swelled up from lovemaking, and rosy red; and there it was right in front of his face. As I was kneeling over him a thick drop of white sperm slid out of me and fell on to the side of his mouth.

"I know some men don't relish the idea of kissing their wife's vagina right after they've been making love. They expect their wife to swallow down every drop of their sperm, but they don't care for the taste of it themselves. But Bill was great. He knew that I was making an effort to make our relationship sexier, and he entered into the spirit of it, you know?

"He held my thighs in his hands, and he lowered me down on to his mouth, and he licked all around my clitoris. I opened up my lips for him, really stretched them apart, so that my clitoris stuck out; and there was the tip of his tongue wriggling its way all the way around it.

"Then he stuck his tongue right into my vagina, right up the hole, and there was his sperm and my lubrication all mixed together, running down his chin. He licked my clitoris faster and faster, and all I could do was close my eyes. My legs were trembling with the strain of it. But I had such a feeling rising up between my legs that I thought that I was someplace else, not in Austin at all.

"When I came, I was gripping the bedrail so tight that my knuckles were white. My stomach tightened, and I was quaking. My vagina kept contracting, again and again, and I squeezed out the last of Bill's sperm. Bill kept his mouth over my vagina the whole time I was coming, and if there's a feeling that's anything like paradise, that has to be it.

"Of course the great part about it was that Bill had gotten all turned on again. When I climbed off him and lay back on the bed, he got on top of me and fucked me for a second time. A great big thrusting fuck that I absolutely adored. I didn't come that time. I sort of half-came—you know, little shudders, but believe me, I didn't mind at all.

"Now, Bill knows what I need; and I hope I understand what he needs, too. Our sex life is so much more exciting and so much more open. If he wants me to wear anything specially sexy, I'll try it. I wore a garter belt and stockings to bed once, and we both took one look at me and burst out laughing. Didn't work! But when I wore a baby-doll nightie, he liked it. And for some reason he likes me nude except for just little white socks.

"We watch blue videos, too, sometimes. Bill likes magazines, but they don't do anything for me. They're mostly women with their legs open, and if I want to see a women with her legs open all I have to do is look in the mirror. I like the videos because you can see men's hard-ons waving around, and you can watch them disappearing into women's vaginas just like some magic trick, and I can imagine it's happening to me."

I am occasionally met with disbelief that ordinary people can talk with such candor about their sex lives and their intimate fantasies and desires. But of course, anybody who has worked in the field of sex guidance will tell you that almost everybody is fascinated by sex, almost everybody has a thousand unanswered questions about sex, and that, given confidentiality and competent questioning, they are only too ready to discuss everything in uncompromising detail. Much of the reason for this is that they are seeking reassurance that their own sexual desires are reasonably normal; and also trying to find out whether they are making the best of their sex lives.

As far as I'm concerned (and my view is shared by a great many doctors and counselors and sex researchers) the only rules about sex are (a)that you and whoever you're doing it with should both enjoy it; that (b)neither of you should do anything just before you've been hurt or threatened or browbeaten, or out of a sense of guilt; and that (c)you should never do anything which causes physical or mental damage. There's one more proviso, of course; and that is that you shouldn't break the law.

You and your lover should have discussed your clitoris and your clitoral responses quite fully. Make sure that you've *told* him how you feel when he touches it; and shown him how to touch it the way that you like best. If you like, you can both have a glass of wine. If you like, he can add to the flavor of his wine by licking your vulva. It should be moist now, and well-prepared for his further exploration.

7

Heaven's Gates: Your Doors To Nightly Delight

Not too long ago, I asked a twenty-three-year-old woman artist to draw me a diagram of the female vulva for a book that I was writing. She called me after an hour in amazement. "I've just examined myself, so that I can get the diagram right, and I've discovered where I pee from, for the very first time."

She had just found her urethral opening—that small hole about an inch-and-a-half below your clitoris from which you urinate.

Although these days I usually find that most women are fairly familiar with their sexual anatomy, I still come across women who never knew that they urinated out of a different hole from the one they use for making love, and (without undertaking a ten-million-dollar nationwide survey) I'd still guess that a large percentage of men *certainly* don't know—although the appearance of detailed photographs in today's men's magazines has gone a long way to demystifying the female vulva.

Many women derive erotic pleasure from touching their urethra as they masturbate, and I have frequently heard of women introducing objects such as bobby-pins or Vaseline-coated cotton-swabs into their urethral opening in order to stimulate themselves sexually.

However, I cannot emphasize strongly enough

161

that you should *never* insert anything into your urethra. The tissues inside are extremely delicate, and
there is an unacceptable risk of infection or injury.
Similarly, you should never insert anything into
your lover's penis.

What *can* be both pleasurable and safe, however,
is to have your lover gently probe your urethral
opening with the tip of his tongue. Try it for a while
during your Mutual Discovery Session . . . not
briefly, but with all the delicacy and unhurried
enjoyment of the ancient Chinese love-technique
known as Tasting the Morning Dew.

Contrary to those fussy women's hygiene advertisements, many men are aroused by the aroma and
the taste of fresh urine on their partner's vulvas.
Here, for instance, is Carla, a twenty-five-year-old
grade school teacher from Providence, R.I.: "I was
also brought up the super-clean American way.
Showers, deodorants, douches, you name it. But
about a year after we started living together, my
boyfriend Jack and I went for a picnic in the woods.
We had a great spread—smoked chicken, pizzas,
and lots of white wine. In fact we had so much
white wine that I had to go into the woods and take
a pee. When I came back I sat down on the rug
again, next to Jack. I didn't realize that my skirt
was way up, and that he could see my panties. He
reached out and touched them, and when I looked
down I realized there was a damp patch on them.
I wasn't really embarrassed. We'd been living
together long enough not to be embarrassed about
things like that. After all, I'd held his head all night
once when he was sick. But Jack touched that damp
patch with his fingers, and then he slowly started
to tug off my panties.

"If I hadn't had so much wine, then maybe I
wouldn't have let him do it. But he took my panties

right off and pushed me gently back on the rug with my skirt way up to my waist. It was a beautiful warm day, and I could feel the breeze and the sunshine between my legs.

"He knelt down and he started to lick me. It wasn't even so much like licking, it was more like *lapping*, you know, like a cat. I could feel the wetness of his tongue, and the breeze made it even more exciting. He looked up at me, and he said, 'You know something, you taste incredible. You taste tangy. You taste like a woman for a change.'

"We made love then, in the open air. I kissed Jack and I could taste myself; and there wasn't anything terrible or disgusting about it; it was just the taste of two people sharing each other completely. These days, I scarcely ever use a vaginal douche. I've read that they lower your resistance to infection, in any case. I'll often come to bed right after I've been for a pee, without wiping myself, and Jack adores it."

We have been told for so long that the ideal person is odorless that we wrinkle up our noses at the thought of human aromas. For sure, personal hygiene is essential in any intimate relationship, for safety as well as for aesthetic purposes. But the fact is that we are highly attuned to sexual aromas, and we respond to them dramatically—the smell of a woman's vaginal secretions, when she's aroused; the smell of a man's penis, rearing out of his shorts; the smell of fresh urine; and the smell of freshly-ejaculated semen.

Lydia, thirty-one, a fashion-store owner from Queens, New York, said: "There is no pleasure that compares with sitting on the toilet the morning after you've been making love to the man you love, and smelling his sperm."

If you've been brought up to have a rather delicate view of sex and sexual relationships, you may find these responses distasteful, if not shocking. But your sex life can only be more fulfilling and more exciting if you take risks with your own inhibitions. In other words—start trying those things that you never thought you'd have the nerve to try.

In spite of the enormous embarrassment that many men and women feel about adventurous sexual activities, the wonderful thing is that they can't hurt you, and they could give you the most explosive physical experience you've ever had in your life.

During this Mutual Discovery Session, don't be afraid to say anything to your partner. Don't be afraid to "talk dirty." Don't be afraid to try anything, either. Even if you decide that a particular sexual act doesn't do anything for you, and you don't want to do it again, it can't hurt you (provided, of course, you follow the golden rules of sexual behavior which I mentioned before.)

Be daring. It won't hurt. Say all of those things that you always wanted to say. Talk about all of those fantasies—even if you don't actually want to act them out. In the throes of sexual excitement, many people have very extreme erotic thoughts—thoughts which they are far too embarrassed to mention in a normal and unexcited frame of mind. However, if they ever dared to describe these thoughts out loud, they could give their lover the key to arousing them even more intensely.

Let's take up this discussion later. But for now, it's worth remembering the words of the marriage ceremony, which can apply equally to anybody who has committed themselves to a long-term sexual relationship: "With my body I thee worship." And that means *all* of your body, in every way that can bring pleasure and happiness and mutual satisfaction.

Now your lover has reached your vagina . . . and by now it should be moist and well-lubricated and ready for his exploration. If you're nervous, and your nervousness has made you dry; or if you've had any difficulty with lubrication, using a clear lubricating jelly like KY is a perfectly acceptable substitute. In fact, it's worth keeping a tube of KY on hand for sexual lubrication, since times often arise when even the most passionate of lovers needs a little help.

Allow your lover to open your vaginal lips and look into your vagina itself. In its normal state, your vagina looks as if it's closed, with the front and back walls meeting. On average, the length of a woman's vagina is about three-and-a-half inches—with the front wall being about an inch shorter than the back wall.

The narrower lower part of your vagina is known (in rather *Guns & Ammo* parlance) as the "vaginal barrel," while the wider part above it is known as the "vaginal vault." The neck of your womb extends into the vault about a half-an-inch. If your lover slips two fingers right up into your vagina, he will be able to feel it. Some women are deeply sexually stimulated if their lovers take hold of the neck of their womb during foreplay and actually move their wombs around. Others find it far too physically disturbing.

Top and bottom of the neck of the womb, there are two spaces, known as *fornices*. The back fornix (feel it) is deeper than the front fornix; and it is into this space that the erect penis normally penetrates during sexual intercourse.

In developing girls, the opening of the vagina is partly closed by a crescent-shaped membrane called the *hymen*, sometimes known as the maidenhead. The hymen usually used to be broken when a girl first had sexual intercourse, which led to all kinds of absurd wedding-night rituals, such as the inspection of the bridal sheets for signs of blood to "prove" that the bride had been a virgin. Most girls used to take the precaution of pricking themselves with a pin to supply the necessary "proof," since the hymen can often be broken well before the first act of intercourse—by strenuous exercise, by masturbation with any kind of phallic object, or (these days, and most commonly) by the use of sanitary tampons.

Occasionally the hymen is thicker, and has to be gradually stretched by repeated acts of intercourse. There are rare cases where the hymen is so thick that a minor surgical cut has to be made before a girl can comfortably have sex.

Allow your lover to feel the walls of your vagina. Normally, the lining of your vagina in its resting state is pink and slightly moist. A certain amount of moisture is always present, but when you get turned on (as you should be now) the moisture increases many times over. In some women, it's practically a flood.

"Whenever I used to kiss my boyfriend, I used to wet my pantyhose. He would feel my breasts, and then he would try to run his hand up my dress, but I never used to let him because I was so embarrassed. I used to get home after a date, and the whole of my pussy was wet, and my pantyhose were wet, and sometimes it even used to run down my legs. It wasn't until a friend showed me your book that I realized I was perfectly normal and that it was girls who *didn't* get wet who had the problem. I started letting my boyfriend touch me between my legs, and he was actually turned on because I was so wet. He used to love sliding his hand down the front of my pantyhose and cupping my pussy in his hand and just kind of squishing it, and then slipping his middle finger right up inside me."

"I'm what you might call 'in between husbands.' I go through phases when I feel incredibly sexy, and I think about sex all the time. By the end of the day, my panties are usually damp. So it's pretty obvious that sexual arousal in your brain causes lubrication in your vagina. I think it's wonderful, part of the wonder of being a woman. My mother would never talk about anything like that. I don't think my mother knew that wet panties existed. She had five children, but she never had an orgasm, not in thirty-four years of marriage. Can you believe that? Just after Micky and I got divorced, I told her that part of his problem was that he hardly ever waited for me to come. She said, 'I always thought he was so punctual.' I tried to explain 'come' and it turned out she didn't know what I meant. My father had never brought her to orgasm, never. And sure as hell she'd never walked around with wet panties feeling good about it."

First of all, it used to be thought that vaginal lubricating fluid poured out of the womb during sexual excitement and flowed down the vaginal walls. Then came the theory that it was produced by a pair of glands called Bartholin's glands, which have their outlets on the inner sides of the vaginal lips. Thomas Bartholin was a brilliant seventeenth-century Danish anatomist who was the first to discover the lymphatic system; so it's rather a pity that he's generally known for two glands in the female vulva that don't actually appear to do anything particularly useful.

Lately, special cameras inserted into women's vaginas now show that the vaginal lubricating fluid is produced by the walls of the vagina itself. Almost as soon as you're aroused, the walls of your vaginal barrel start to "sweat" droplets of lubricant, which join together to form a smooth and glistening lining of lubricant, ready to smoothe the way for your lover's penis.

Other changes take place in your vagina in readiness for sex. As I said in *More Ways to Drive Your Man Wild in Bed*: "Your vagina is just as magical and just as complicated as your lover's penis. In fact, it is much *more* versatile. Just because it happens to be internal rather than dangling around outside, that doesn't mean that it isn't beautiful and positive and that it doesn't have a shape and a form and an aesthetic quality all its own.

"Think of your vagina as a shape in itself: a shape that changes when you become sexually aroused, just as the shape of a man's penis changes. You never think of your mouth as being negative—as just a "hole"—so why should you think of your vagina that way? Especially when it's such an independent, flexible organ, capable of giving such pleasure to you and to the man you love."

And as a recent medical review remarked: "It is strange that for so long the vagina was regarded as being simply an inert tube connecting the uterus with the vulva, and that its exact functioning during sexual intercourse was unsuspected. It is only modern developments in the field that have enabled us to realize just how complex its workings are, and how very much more it is than simply a 'sheath' for the male sexual organ."

As you prepare to receive your lover's penis, the upper two-thirds of the vaginal barrel actually increase in length, and your vagina widens. In the resting state, the front and back walls of the vagina are in contact, but as you become increasingly aroused, they seperate. The muscles of your vagina expand and relax without any conscious effort on your part, until finally your vaginal barrel is enlarged almost into a balloon shape.

At the same time, the neck of your womb lifts itself and moves forward, so that there is more room in the vaginal vault for your lover's penis to enter. Your vaginal walls change color . . . from innocent pink to passionate purple.

One question I'm often asked, especially by younger girls: "I'm quite small and my boyfriend is really big. How can I possibly fit him inside me?"

The answer: No matter how small you are—provided you have reached a high state of sexual arousal—your vagina is elastic enough to accommodate the largest penis you can imagine. As one perky young lady from Los Angeles commented: "All I have to do now is find the largest penis that I can imagine."

Open your vagina as wide as you can with your fingers and let your lover see it, touch it, explore it. Just as he has shared his penis with you, share your vagina with him.

Your vagina is composed of two layers—the inner lining, which is soft and moist; and an outer, thicker layer of muscle fibers. The thin inner lining rises up into two ridges on the front and back walls of your vaginal barrel. Interestingly, these ridges show where the two sides of the vagina met and fused together when you were developing as a fetus in your mother's womb. Technically, these ridges are known as the *columns* of the vagina.

Fanning out on either side of these columns are numerous corrugated folds known as *rugae*. These are most pronounced on younger women and tend to disappear in later life, especially if you've had children. After your menopause—the so-called "change of life"—the inner walls of your vagina may be completely smooth.

Show your lover which kind of vaginal massage you like the best. Show him how he can insert his index finger into your vagina and press it gently upward and forward to put internal pressure on your clitoris—your 'G-Spot.'

Some women enjoy two or three or even more fingers inserted into their vagina simultaneously. A few are highly aroused by the strong stimulation of having their lover's entire hand inside them.

Gina, a thirty-three-year-old jewelry store assistant from Philadelphia, Pa., said: "I've always liked my lovemaking to be very vigorous and forceful, you know. Lots of rolling around and screaming and biting. It turns me on, that kind of high-tension atmosphere. It makes it seem like it's dangerous, even though it isn't. Steve was the first one who ever fist-fucked me. We'd been to a promotional party, and I think I'd drunk too much champagne, so by the time we got back to my apartment I was very giggly and amorous. We collapsed straight on to the couch and started kissing and mauling.

"I remember I was wearing this very shiny green silk evening-gown. Steve slid it right up over my hips, and while we were kissing, he slipped his hand inside my pantyhose and started to massage my cunt. After a while, he really started to turn me on, and I kept lifting my hips and pressing my clitoris harder against his hand. I said, 'Fuck me,' but he just grinned and kissed me and kept on massaging me with his fingers.

"He slipped one finger right up inside my cunt, as far as it would go, right up to the knuckle. Now I was *really* getting excited, and I started biting his lips and biting his shoulder and begging him to fuck me. I even tried to open up his fly. I could feel his cock through his evening pants. It was sticking up hard and solid and all I wanted was to have that cock inside me. But he twisted sideways so that I couldn't reach his cock, and he kept on kissing me and nuzzling my neck and working his finger up inside me.

"I was very juicy by then; and he slipped another finger up my cunt, two fingers, and kept wriggling them and waggling them, until I was almost ready to scream. Then he pushed three fingers in, and then four. Four fingers right up inside me, massaging my cunt, so that when I looked down, all I could see was his thumb going around and around on my clitoris.

"Then he drew his hand out of me, not all the way, but most of the way, and folded his thumb across the palm of his hand, like this. He gave me this long deep kiss, with his tongue almost halfway down my throat. And at the same time he pushed his whole hand gradually into my cunt, real gradual, so that he didn't hurt me. It was amazing. I was so turned on that I was gasping. My legs were wide open, and there was his wrist, with my cunt lips tight around it, so his whole hand was right up inside me.

"He held the neck of my womb in his fingertips. The first time he touched it, it made me jump. But then he gradually massaged it around and around, and I felt like he was slowly churning my whole body around.

"I had an orgasm that came from someplace really different, like the back of my brain or someplace like that. I felt like I was going through an earthquake, or a storm at sea. It was definitely one of those orgasms that rate about nine on the Richter scale. I think I blacked out. Well, maybe, I didn't black out. But when it was over, and I opened my eyes, I felt like I was opening my eyes on a new planet that I'd never visited before."

There are scores of different ways in which your vagina can be stimulated during lovemaking. To begin with, many women are reticent about inserting "alien objects" like vibrators or dildos into their vaginas. But if you use sex toys sensibly, you can vary your lovemaking enormously—and at the same time make sure that you enjoy the very highest level of stimulation.

The choice of vaginal stimulants available in sex stores and by mail order is absolutely staggering. If you could afford them all, you could probably use a different vaginal stimulant six times a week, fifty-two weeks of the year, and never have to use the same one twice.

The old favorite is the torpedo-shaped hard plastic vibrator, powered by batteries. It operates by spinning an eccentric metal weight, thus creating the same *brrrrrrrr* kind of effect as a car-wheel which hasn't been properly balanced.

But the variations on this theme are almost limitless. You can buy sets of different heads for attaching to this basic vibrator—pointed, mushroom-shaped, pepper-pot shaped. And you can buy soft latex sleeves to fit over them so that they look and feel like erect male penises, complete with bulging veins. There's even a "G-Spot" vibrator with a curved extension which is intended to act like a furiously-massaging finger.

There are huge, oversized vibrating dildos—such as the Jumbo, described as "eleven inches of solid curved rampant dildo, vibrating inches of veined realism"—or a two-pronged dildo called Double The Pleasure, with one fat penis-shape and one thin penis-shape for simultaneous vaginal and anal vibration.

There are dildos that vibrate up and down as well as round and round. There are dildos that heat up—the Hot Stud, which "heats the tip to erect penis temperature." There are jellyfish dildos, dildos with all kinds of clitoral stimulators attached, and even dildos that glow in the dark so that you can watch your vagina light up.

There's a Leetle Spanish Bully Boy—"if you'd like an ever-willing erect pocket pal then this is for you m'lady"—and a Testi Bully Boy which is designed "with a super-large testicle scrotum for those who like something to squeeze and get hold of."

The Ben-Wa, or love-balls, have been on the market almost since the beginning of mass-market sex-toys. These are two weighted plastic balls, connected by a cord, which you insert in your vagina at any time you like (even when you're off to work), and are supposed to massage you continuously during the day. They're based on an ancient Chinese sex-toy, but none of the reports I've heard about them are very enthusiastic.

I've had much better reports on three very new sex-toys. The first is Joni's Butterfly, which has recently topped the best-seller list as the favorite U.S. stimulator. It's a latex pad with soft brush-like bristles on it, rather like a miniature rubber bathmat. This device is activated by a vibrating electric motor. The unique selling-point is that Joni's Butterfly is strapped into position with thin, discreet straps "allowing no escape." I have yet to meet any woman who has tried wearing it under her clothes, but obviously it could be done.

Another excellent stimulator is Heather's Heart, a soft heart-shape made out of latex, with similar brush-like protrusions on it. The Heart is held in place by an erect shaft "all covered with silky soft spikes of jelly latex" which you insert into your vagina, holding the bristles close to your clitoris. Again, this device is operated by a vibrator.

Anal stimulators have undergone a technological transformation, too. A few years ago, no open mention was made in sex-toy catalogs of devices to stimulate the nerves in the anus. Especially slender vibrators were marketed "for intimate probing," but that was as far as it went. Currently, there are several excellent new devices available which have been specifically designed for anal stimulation. This makes them far safer and much more satisfying. Some of them can be inserted into your anus during lovemaking, giving both you and your lover a high degree of additional stimulus without interfering with normal intercourse.

Many vibrators offer a slender extension which can be inserted into the anus. But probably the best anal stimulator is the new Butt Plug, a conical vibrator with a short neck around which the anal muscles can tighten during stimulation, but also a wide base that obviates any risk of losing it inside your rectum.

Another firm rule, remember: never insert anything into your anus which isn't completely clean, perfectly harmless in texture and shape, and which can't be easily extracted. Every doctor has stories of patients who have lost the most extraordinary objects up their rectums; ranging from candles, to bars of soap, to drinking-glasses. Sometimes these objects can only be removed by major surgery.

Vaginal and anal stimulation can be both exciting and beneficial . . . provided you use sex-toys that are specifically designed for the purpose.

Quite a considerable number of women have found that—far from being hideously unnatural—a vibrating dildo is a considerable help in reviving their sex lives. One woman wrote to me and called her dildo "the lover I always wanted—silent, willing, and always stiff." If you decide to try a vibrating dildo, you'll have to take care how you introduce it into your sex life, particularly if your lover or husband has been having difficulty in maintaining an erection or in satisfying you often enough.

The critical thing to do is to make your lover feel that the dildo was *his* idea, and that it belongs to him. He should see it as an extension of his own virility, not as a sly gibe about his lack of prowess. Only you can be the judge of how your lover will take to the introduction of a bodyless penis into your bed, but on the whole, men are not averse to sex-toys, and if you use it diplomatically, he should soon begin to regard it as his friend.

Intelligently incorporated into a sexual relationship, a vibrating dildo can relieve your lover of the anxiety of not being able to maintain an erection; or not being able to satisfy you as often as he would like.

Here's Gaye, a twenty-eight-year-old orchestral musician from Pasadena, California: "Both Rick and I are musicians, and we both work real hard. We started living together because we shared such a feeling for music. Our relationship wasn't sexual at first, but then we gradually fell in love, and one night after a tremendous opening night, we got drunk and went to bed together for the first time.

"Our sex life hasn't been easy. For one thing Rick is tremendously talented, very highly strung. The slightest setback during the day, and he can't get it together in bed. It's not that he doesn't love me. I know that he *does* love me. He finds me sexy, too. But once he starts feeling stressed, he can't make love to me properly; and when he can't make love to me properly, he gets even more stressed.

"I was talking to one of the women in the orchestra about sex and how she got along. She had it even harder than me; her husband was away on tour for three or four months at a stretch. She said that when she was younger, she used to have affairs when he was away, but then her husband found out and practically divorced her. She said she masturbated with a vibrator. She said that it wasn't as good as a real man, no way—but it kept her calm, and it was better than nothing, and better than risking her marriage. Another thing was she didn't feel guilty because her husband knew about it, and he didn't feel threatened. It was only an eight-inch piece of plastic, after all.

"She showed me a mail-order catalog, and I decided that maybe I should try a vibrator for myself. But first of all I went to Rick and told him all about it. I acted all shy and asked him whether he thought it would be a good idea. He tried to act all cool, but to tell you the truth I don't think that he could believe his luck. He obviously thought it was a real turn-on. He said, sure, go ahead, let's order one, and so I did. A big one, ten inches long and about three inches wide, really huge, and bright blue, too, so that Rick could take it as kind of a joke. In other words, I didn't want him to feel that I was looking for a cock like his, only hard instead of soft. I didn't want to put him down. I wanted him to feel that I was looking for some totally new kind of sexual thrill altogether.

"When the package arrived I was so excited that I could hardly wait for Rick to come home. I let him open it up, and when he took it out of the box he laughed his head off to begin with. I mean, apart from being blue, it was *enormous*. It was more like a donkey's cock than a man's. In fact, neither of us could stop laughing. Maybe it was nerves, maybe it was embarrassment. But I could see that the idea of my pushing this monster up inside my pussy was a turn-on; and it didn't surprise me when he suggested we go to bed early and try it out.

"To tell you the truth, I almost lost my nerve. But Rick suddenly seemed to have found a whole lot of fresh confidence. He took off my T-shirt for me, and unbuttoned my jeans. He hadn't undressed me like that for as long as I could remember. He laid me down on the bed and stripped off his own clothes. His cock looked really big and hard, and I took it in my fist and rubbed it up and down a few times. After about the third rub, a drop of juice came out of the end of his cock, and so I rubbed it again and squeezed out some more.

"He kissed me, and touched my breasts, and made love to me the way he used to make love to me when we first dated. He didn't seem to be panicking any more. How can I put it? He seemed to be back in control. And of course the whole point was that he wasn't worried that he couldn't last long enough to make me come.

"We made love, just plain simple ordinary beautiful intercourse. Him on top, me underneath. He was hard, and he was sexy, and I adored every second of it. He almost managed to make me come. I was trembling right on the edge. But I do find it difficult to reach an orgasm. It takes a whole lot of really intense stimulation, and I'm one of those people who's easily distracted when they're making love. You know what I mean—I only have to hear a noise outside, or a door banging, and it puts me right back to square one.

"But he was really good. And there isn't anything more beautiful than looking down and seeing the man you love going in and out of you, and feeling him right up inside your cunt.

"He came. He couldn't stop himself. But as soon as he'd come, he didn't hesitate. He took that huge dildo from the nightstand, and he said, 'Now it's *your* turn.'

"He opened my legs wider, and he pressed the head of the dildo up against my cunt, and rolled it around so that it was slick with cunt-juice and sperm. Then he opened my cunt with his fingers as wide as he could. I was gasping by then. I felt all breathless and excited, like the whole world was disappearing underneath me. My cunt was swimming with sperm, which made it much easier. Rick pushed this blue dildo into me, a little at a time, and I could feel my cunt being stretched. It was a really strange sensation the first time. Very erotic, but strange. But because Rick was doing it, because it was part of something we were doing together, it wasn't at all embarrassing or dirty, if you understand what I mean. He enjoyed doing it, and I enjoyed him doing it to me.

"He slowly forced that whole huge donkey-sized dildo right up inside me; and at the same time he was quickly rubbing my clitoris with his fingers. I sat up to watch him at first. It was really extraordinary to watch this massive blue cock disappearing inside my cunt. I couldn't believe that I could take it all. in. But then this incredible feeling began to come over me, and I had to lie back on the bed and close my eyes. He pushed the dildo in and out like a really slow fuck. When it was right up inside me, it felt like it was too big—but when he took it out I desperately wanted it back in again. And all the time he kept rubbing my clitoris faster and faster.

"I reached out and took hold of Rick's cock. It was still sticky and wet from fucking me. While he pushed the dildo in and out of me, I rubbed him, too, and after a little while he started to get stiff again.

"Toward the end, I was panting. He switched on the dildo's vibrator, and that was all I needed. I can't describe the feeling, I wish I could. It was unbelievable. I was shaking like a leaf. And when I'd stop shaking, Rick slid the dildo out of me, and lifted my leg, and slid his own cock back into me, from the side.

"He gave a few quick thrusts, and he came for a second time, which was amazing. And that night we did it for a third time, too, just before morning.

"These days, we hardly ever use the dildo. Rick doesn't have trouble getting hard any more—well, not very much. And if he does, he knows he can always give me an orgasm by using King Kong."

Gaye's use of a dildo was intelligent, creative and positive. Not that you have to have a sexual problem to enjoy dildos or any other kind of sex-toy. Even if you've never considered buying a sex-toy before, it's both interesting and mind-broadening to look through a catalog of what erotic devices modern technology has to offer. You can usually find advertisements for sex-toy merchandising houses in the classified pages of men's magazines like *Playboy* and *Penthouse*.

Sex-toys open the door to a whole variety of different sexual sensations and can give both you and your lover the incentive to make love more frequently. Susie, a thirty-six-year-old dancer from Seattle, Washington, said: "Both my husband and I get a tremendous kick out of having sex with an anal vibrator inserted. You can have normal intercourse, but at the same time the inside of your ass is buzzing with this amazingly sexy tingle."

Anal stimulation is one of the ways in which you can make sure that you have sex not only six times a week, but fifty-two weeks of the year. Although many women are reluctant to try it, it can be a highly arousing substitute for vaginal sex during your menstrual periods—provided you take certain essential precautions, and provided you're well-prepared for it.

Your lover should now take his finger out of your vagina, and take it downward to your anus, so that he is touching your anal sphincter—the ring of muscle—with his fingertip.

Unless you already have frequent experience with anal sex, the natural reaction of your anal sphincter will be to contract tightly, to prevent admission of your lover's finger. But if you consciously push your muscles *against* his fingertip, your sphincter will open and (with sufficient lubrication) he should be able to slide his finger inside.

The main objections that women have to anal sex is that they're afraid it might be dirty, and that it hurts.

As far as hygiene is concerned, there is rarely any fecal matter in the lower part of your rectum until you are just about to pass it; so a finger or a penis can be inserted as deep as it will go and still remain unsoiled. That isn't to say that the rectum doesn't contain virulent bacteria. It does—and both you and your lover must take certain simple and basic measures to make sure that anal sex is a pleasure rather than a source of infection and irritation.

Whether it's a finger, a penis or a vibrator, never insert anything into your vagina after it has been in your rectum without thoroughly washing it first. Some of the most persistent of vaginal infections are caused by men who start lovemaking by inserting their penises into their partner's anuses and then switch to the vagina in order to climax. If your lover starts by making love to you anally, then he must either stop and wash himself before he inserts his penis into your vagina, or (preferably) he should continue to make love to you anally and ejaculate into your rectum.

You and your lover should always wash your hands thoroughly after anal sex, paying particular attention to your fingernails.

Never have unprotected anal intercourse with anybody, man or woman, unless you are absolutely certain that they are HIV-negative. And I mean one-hundred-one percent certain. If you're pretty sure but not entirely sure, use a condom.

While those stipulations may sound rather doomy, they don't really involve much more than the precautions you would normally take when having vaginal intercourse. And apart from allowing you to continue lovemaking during your period, anal sex can widen your erotic experience far beyond your normal horizons.

Anal sex has an ancient and venerable history. Aside from its obvious popularity among homosexuals, it is described and recommended in many Indian and Chinese marriage books, either as a substitute for vaginal intercourse during menstruation, or as an extra stimulus for a man's penis when his wife's vagina has lost its elasticity through repeated childbirth. But of course it can be much more than that: it can also be a refreshingly different kind of erotic stimulus for couples who are looking for something new.

Anal intercourse can also be completely painless: provided you both understand that your anus is not naturally designed to accept an erect penis, and that you will need a little self-training and a great deal of lubricant to make it pleasurable and successful.

The best way to educate your body for anal sex is to start by soaping your index finger every time you take a bath or a shower, and inserting it into your anus as far as it will go—working it around and around so that you can feel the lining of your rectum. After you can easily do that you can try inserting one of the specially-designed anal stimulators that are attached to vibrators, well-lubricated with Vaseline or KY, or a long, slender candle—provided you make absolutely sure that you always leave four or five inches protruding from your anus, so that you can always withdraw it.

You will find that your sphincter soon learns to open rather than close when you touch it with a finger or a phallic object. You will be able to insert two or three fingers into your anus quite easily, and then a full-size vibrator. Don't force anything further up your rectum if it makes you feel uncomfortable.

The classic description of anal training appears in Pauline's Reage's *Story of O*. O's captors decide that her anus is too tight, and "thereafter, for eight days in succession . . . O wore, inserted in her anus and held in place by three little chains attached to a leather belt encircling her haunches, held, that is to say, in such a manner that the play of her internal muscles was unable to dislodge it, an ebonite rod fashioned in the shape of an uprisen male sex. Thus was she spread, and spread wider every day, for every day . . . whoever else happened to be there introduced a thicker one. At the end of a week, there was no further need of an instrument, and her lover told O he was happy that she was now doubly open."

Kathy, a twenty-two-year-old receptionist from Atlanta, also found that anal sex doubled her fun. "My boyfriend Paul had always liked to slip his finger up my ass when we were making love, and sometimes I used to do it to him, too. About a year ago, we were lying in bed together, and Paul began to get particularly horny. I was reading a book, but I could feel his stiff cock right up against my bare back. The trouble was, I was right in the middle of my period, and there was nothing much I could do, except maybe give him head or masturbate him. But I was horny, too, and I didn't feel like doing anything one-sided that was going to end up with my being more frustrated than ever.

"Paul started caressing my back and then my bottom. I told him to stop, but he carried on. He parted the cheeks of my bottom and touched my asshole. Then he licked his finger and gradually corkscrewed his finger up inside my ass. At the same time, he reached around and started to stroke my clitoris.

"At first, I couldn't make up my mind whether I liked what was going on, but gradually I began to enjoy that feeling of having something right up my asshole. It felt kind of strange and sexy and weird. I didn't say anything, but I didn't push him away, and I raised my knees a little higher so that he could push his finger further.

"Having a man make love to your ass is one of those things that you have to be right in the mood for. If you don't feel like it, it's a pain and you can't enjoy it. But if you do feel like it, if you really feel like opening yourself up, it's amazing. It's completely different from normal lovemaking.

"Paul reached over to the table beside the bed and took out a tube of KY. We used to use it when I came off the pill for a while, and Paul had to wear condoms. He squeezed a whole blob of it over the end of his cock and smothered my asshole with it, sticking his finger up so that I was well lubricated. It was cold, that KY, and it made me shiver. But then I felt his hot cock right up against my asshole, and I felt this terrible excitement that I was actually going to be fucked in the ass. It was like being frightened and turned on, both at the same time.

"I didn't know how I was going to get him inside me. At first my asshole kept closing up tight, and he couldn't force himself into me, no matter how hard he tried. But then he said, 'push me away, push me away,' and of course my asshole opened right up then, and he pushed the whole of the head of his cock inside.

"His cock felt huge. My muscles kept twitching and flinching, but Paul shushed me, and told me to relax, and then to push against him again. I took a deep breath, and pushed. To be quite frank, it felt like having a really big, deeply satisfying crap. I know that sounds terrible, but there's something of that kind of pleasure in it, only the feeling goes on and on.

"Paul lifted my leg over and turned me on to my back so that my feet were up in the air. He fucked me very slowly in and out, small strong pushes. I could feel his balls against my bottom, and his pubic hair all around my ass. When I raised my head I could see his cock right up to the hilt in my asshole, and my cunt gaping open. He pushed and pushed, and then I had an orgasm. It wasn't a huge orgasm. It didn't feel like any orgasm I've ever had before. It seemed to ripple right through my ass and in between my thighs. Maybe it was nothing more than a sort of nervous spasm, but whatever it was, it was delicious.

"It took only two or three more pushes, and then Paul came too. He gripped me so tight, you wouldn't believe it. I could feel his sperm like a small warm flood up my ass. He slowly took out his cock, and it was bright red, just like my asshole.

I flexed my muscles, and sperm rose out of my asshole, and ran into my cunt.

"As I said, there are times when you don't feel like having it up the ass, no matter what. You just don't feel like it. In some ways, it's more personal than having it the usual way. But sometimes I don't want anything else. Sometimes I want to be raunchy and rude and show Paul that he can have all of me."

Your anus is very flexible, but you should treat it with great respect. *Deep Throat* star Linda Lovelace claimed that she had trained her anus so well that she could take two penises inside it simultaneously. And the extreme of anal stimulation is known as "fist-fucking"—a predominantly homosexual practise in which one man inserts his whole hand into the anus of another, sometimes right up to the middle of the forearm.

But if you can accept your lover's fingers and occasionally his erect penis into your anus, then that will be quite enough to have proved yourself to be a highly versatile and adventurous lover.

Remember, though . . . if you've tried it, and you really don't like it, then you're under no obligation. Simply explain to your lover that it's not for you. And that applies to every sexual variation. Sexual excitement has to be mutual and sympathetic, and no sexual relationship can be heightened and intensified if one partner is suffering in silence.

We have reached the climax of the Mutual Discovery Session. By now you will have realized that by going over all the basics of sexual discovery and exploring some of the possibilities of sexual stimulation, you know everything that you will ever need to know about your partner's responses, and how to create the framework of an arousing and well-refreshed relationship.

Now, you deserve to make love. Still slowly, remember! Still savoring every moment of it. And if it isn't one of the closest and most satisfying times that you've ever had together, then I'll want to know why.

8

So Many Ways . . . So Little Time

If you and your lover make love six days a week, every week of the year, that still means only 312 acts of love from one Thanksgiving to the next. And once you're confident about the basics of good lovemaking, you'll be able to think of far more variations than that. It's a hard life, isn't it?

As we've seen, good lovemaking comes from knowing each other's bodies, being aware of each other's responses, and being alert to each other's particular likes and dislikes.

By playing on each other's fantasies, by varying your techniques, by showing a willingness to try anything and everything that pleases you, you can have the kind of sex life that most people only dream about. Six nights a week, if you feel like it. Even more, if you've got the stamina.

Once you have closely acquainted (or *re-*acquainted) yourselves with each other's bodies and sexual responses . . . once you have openly talked about each other's needs and special desires . . . then you can start working out how to bridge any sexual differences between you, and how to make sure that you're *both* sexually satisfied.

As we discussed in the introduction, some people have far greater sexual urges than others. Some people are far more quickly satisfied. Others—provided they have the warmth and comfort of a stable relationship—can almost take or leave sex; they really don't care about it all that much.

With the aid of my questionnaire, I showed you how you could roughly work out the scale of the sexual differential between you and your partner so that you could both identify how much is needed to be done to bring you closer together.

The Mutual Discovery Session wasn't as simple as it might have appeared. It was very carefully constructed on the lines of some of the most successful modern sex therapy to guide you both not only through all of your *physical* responses, but through many of your most important *emotional* responses, too. If you harbored any major inhibitions about any part of your sexuality, then they would have come out into the open, and you would at least have had the *opportunity* to discuss them with your partner.

It's on the basis of what you've both discovered about yourselves during this session that you can revive your day-to-day (or night-to-night) sex life. Now that you really know what you think and what you want, you are both in a position to be able to do everything possible to please and accommodate your mate.

Remember: if you generally need more frequent sexual satisfaction than your partner, don't be impatient. Work out ways in which your partner can please you without always having to involve him- or herself in a full-scale sexual act. For instance, if your husband or lover rarely seems to want to make love, he should at least bridge that sexual gap by masturbating you or giving you oral sex. If you enjoy them, he may be able to use sex-toys like dildos or vibrators to give you satisfaction. It's his sexual obligation to please you—just as it's *your* sexual obligation to please him.

If you've been brought up to believe that masturbation is terribly wrong, and you've never really had any experience with sex-toys, then I know that you'll find it difficult to consider achieving sexual satisfaction by these methods. But millions of couples very happily and successfully use masturbation in their sex relationships in order to counterbalance a discrepancy in their sexual urges—and I haven't noticed any decline in the worldwide sale of vibrators, so somebody must be using them.

You may even find that your partner is content for you to masturbate yourself. Gina, a thirty-four-year-old homemaker from Wichita, Kansas, wrote: "Ned was a whole lot older than me when we married, and he was never much interested in the sexual side of life. I married him because he was kind and appreciative, and I knew that he would always take care of me. I'd been through two marriages before, and both of my previous husbands had beaten up on me.

"I used to masturbate when Ned was at work. Around coffee-time I used to take off my clothes and lie naked on the couch and just daydream that I was being fucked by all of these young men, one after the other.

"One morning I opened my eyes in the middle of masturbating and Ned was standing there watching me. He'd forgotten his lunch-pail and come back for it. I felt really ashamed and embarrassed, but he was a much more understanding man than I'd given him credit for. He said, 'I know I'm not a fireball in bed, and I don't ever expect to be. But if you want to do that, why not do it when we're together? Because you're my wife, and why should we have secrets, especially about loving, and I sure as hell don't mind.'

"So that's the way we worked it out. When we're

in bed together at night, and I feel horny, I snuggle up to Ned and masturbate myself, and he holds me tight and kisses me, and he shares my satisfaction right alongside of me with no embarrassment and no shame whatsoever. Actually, it's worked out that we seem to make love a whole lot more often, too, because sometimes he's feeling a little horny after I've been masturbating, and he slips himself into me, and I get the best of both worlds."

It's this complete lack of inhibition and embarrassment that's the secret of frequent, creative lovemaking. So many men and women write and say, "I can't tell my husband, but . . ." or "How can I tell my wife that I want to . . ." or "My lover won't listen if I try to explain that . . ."

Men in particular can be stunningly deaf when it comes to discussions about sex. Even today, with so much sexual education available in schools and in books and in magazines, many men feel that each act of sex is some kind of test of their masculine prowess. A woman has only to suggest that her lover might spend a little more time on foreplay, or pay more attention to her breasts, or try a different position, and she'll be met either by stony silence or an explosion of anger.

Of course much of the thrill of the act of love is based on the penetration of a willing woman by a man with a mighty penis. No matter what feminists might say, it would be absurd to suggest otherwise.

But the act of love isn't a baton-charge. No man's prowess in bed has ever been diminished by being alert to his partner's needs—whether she expresses them out loud or whether he's sensitive enough to realize that he could be giving her something a little extra.

So: listen to each other, both of you, openly and

broadmindedly; and make a point of acting on what you learn.

Everybody has particular sexual tastes, and men rather more than women often have a minor fetish . . . such as an interest in erotic underwear, or leather, or rubber . . . and an interest in some of the wilder sexual variations, like bondage, or sado-masochism, or "wet sex."

It will probably take a great deal of diplomatic questioning for you to discover if your lover is interested in any of these variations. But a little sexual experimenting may bring his most deeply-hidden desires to light—and if you can indulge them for him, you'll not only intensify his satisfaction with you as a lover, but you'll probably find that there's plenty of erotic excitement in them for you, too.

I am very specifically *not* talking about men who are unable to achieve sexual arousal unless they are whipped or tied up or dressed in rubber; or unless they are hurting the woman with whom they are having sex. Such men are suffering from sexual and psychological dysfunction, and they need professional guidance.

In a satisfying and creative love-life, one partner's sexual urges should never blot out the other's, and if you happen to find that you're involved in a sexual relationship in which your partner always has to go through a certain sexual ritual in order to achieve a climax, then you should seriously reconsider what you're doing, and whether your partner is in need of clinical help.

This is particularly important when a man always insists on tying you up or being tied up himself, or hurting you in some way, or practising sexual techniques which involve some restriction of breathing. These practices are highly dangerous, and your only response to any man who suggests them is "no way, Jose."

As far as the milder fetishes are concerned, however, they're the colorful, sparkling stuff of which exciting sex relationships are made. Very few men are impervious to the eroticism of sexy underwear, and to give your love life that six-days-a-week scintillation, try buying some really provocative lingerie and wearing nothing else when he comes home tonight.

There used to be a time when the only sexy underwear you could buy was the kind of red-and-black-and-purple nylon froth produced by Lili St. Cyr and Frederick's of Hollywood. I'm not putting it down. More men would like to see their wives and girlfriends wearing peephole bras and sequinned G-strings than you would ever believe.

And, as I say to women time and time again, by dressing in erotic underwear for your own lover in private, you're not behaving like a Jezebel. You're showing that you're proud of your body and the effect it has on him, and that you have a sense of fun and a sexy sense of sharing.

These days, you don't need to send off to a mail-order company for sexy underwear. Like pubic shaving, which I once used to write about as a sexual variation, simple and sexy underwear for women has now become mainstream. You can find the briefest and prettiest of panties and bras in any department store, and in Paris I was recently shown a collection of exquisite embroidered thongs from Switzerland—tiny wisps of highly-expensive lingerie—which elegant European women regard as *de rigueur*, particularly under fitted slacks.

In *The Joy of Sex*, there's a design for a do-it-yourself G-string, but I don't recommend that you try it unless you want to look as if you've suffered a serious injury right where it matters, and you've tried to bandage yourself up. But, based on a make-your-own-sexy-underwear idea that I was given when preparing my previous book *Sex Secrets of the Other Woman*, you could try the ribbon-thong, which looks delightful, as if you've gift-wrapped yourself for the man in your life.

The girl who showed it to me wore one almost all the time so that she was able to create new panties for herself every morning of the week. Her basic design was a broad (2–2½ inch) silk ribbon, two yards long, in any color, although she personally preferred pink and white and (occasionally) black. She started by holding one end of the ribbon against her stomach, about two or three inches above her vagina, then passing it around her waist and tying it in a large flat bow, with one very long end trailing in front. This long end she passed tightly between her legs, folding it between the cheeks of her bottom. She cut it on the bias to prevent fraying, and then cut a three-inch slit in it to make two ends which she could tie around the back. She admitted that it was "more decorative than useful," but said that her lover adored it.

Many men have a taste for garter-belts and stockings, too. Apart from the sensual feeling of nylon-sheathed legs, the erotic appeal seems to be that a woman in stockings is dressed and yet still sexually exposed—whereas a woman in pantyhose is for all intensive purposes covered up. You can overcome this problem, of course, by wearing open-crotch pantyhose, but the classic eroticism of the garter-belt still, quite obviously, endures.

Kelly, a twenty-seven-year-old waitress from Denver, Colorado, bought herself a garter-belt and stockings simply because she thought they looked feminine and attractive. "I always leave for work before my boyfriend Tony because I'm on the early shift, so that morning he didn't see me putting on my stockings. But when he came home that evening, and I was cooking the supper, he came into the kitchen and put his arms around me, and suddenly he could feel my garter-belt through my dress.

"He couldn't believe it. He lifted my dress and he practically flipped. He said, 'You're fantastic! You're so sexy!' He smoothed his hands all over my bare thighs, and slid his fingers down inside my stocking-tops, and then he caressed me in between my legs. I never wear panties, I don't even own any, and he just loved the idea of my walking around with my pussy bare underneath my dress.

"He turned off the stove, and he took me through to the living-room. He picked me up in his arms and laid me on the couch. I was going to kick my shoes off, but he said no. He liked me better with shoes on. He took off his own clothes, all of them, so that he was completely naked. He's quite slim, and his prick was sticking out like the Empire State building.

"He lifted my legs up high, and he took hold of my thighs, running his hands right inside my stocking-tops again, and he pulled me on to him. He was so hard and big, he seemed to go all the way up inside me. His balls were tight, too.

"He fucked me really quickly, like he could hardly control himself. It was only about a minute before he came to a climax. His prick slipped out just as he came, and his jism went everywhere; all over my pubic hair, all over my garter-belt.

"But he didn't stop. He rubbed my pussy with his fingers, massaging all that jism into me, and all round my bottom. It only took me a couple of minutes before I had an orgasm myself. By that time his prick had come up again. He lifted me up so that I was kneeling on the floor in front of the couch, with my dress held up and my bottom exposed, and he fucked me from the back, much slower this time, caressing and stroking my legs.

"I'd never had so much fucking in one half-hour. And when he was about to climax for the second time, he took his prick out of my pussy and slid it down in between my stocking and the side of my thigh. I looked down at it and I could see his big red prick trapped under that shiny black nylon, right up against my leg; and when he came I could actually see the jism spurt out.

"I wear stockings almost all the time now—not only because they turn Tony on so much, but because I like them, too. I like to feel the fresh air between my legs! But I wear them to bed, too. Yes, and high-heeled shoes, too, because Tony finds them exciting; and if he's turned on, then I'm turned on, too."

Tony's erotic response to Kelly's stockings was completely within the bounds of what we describe as "normal sex." Even Ken, a thirty-five-year-old telephone systems engineer from Boise, Idaho, could be described as "normal," although what *he* liked was to wear the stockings and garter-belt himself.

His wife Irene said, "The first time he told me what he wanted to do, I was desperately upset. I thought, oh God, I've married a gay or a transvestite or something. I even went to my doctor and talked to him about it. But my doctor was terrific. He really put my mind at rest. He said that he'd known Ken for years, and there was nothing wrong with Ken at all. He simply wanted to try a new sexual experience. He said lots of men try on their wives' underwear now and again. It doesn't mean they want to dress up as women. It's a way of getting close to their wives' sexuality. In fact, it's more of a compliment than anything else.

"So one evening I said to Ken, 'Come on, why don't you try it?' and he said 'What?' and I said, 'Why don't you try wearing my stockings?' I helped him put them on. I can't honestly say that they turned me on to *look* at. But they turned *him* on, because he got a huge erection, and he wanted to make love to me there and then. When he was actually making love to me, the sensation of his legs in nylon stockings was quite . . . I don't know. It was strange, but it did turn me on, too. I can't explain why.

"It was an effort for me to behave as if Ken was doing something normal. But I managed it, in the end; and now I don't think anything of it. In fact, sometimes I suggest it myself. He's really appreciative, and our sex-life is better than ever. When you come to think about it, where's the harm? All I'm getting out of it is a happier husband, and you can't argue with that. And they're only stockings, after all. It's no worse than me borrowing his socks."

Many men have a mild fetish for women's panties. Read through the classified columns of many men's magazines and you will find advertisements such as "Lady Cyclist Has Used Panties For Sale," or "Soiled Panties, State Requirements." On the whole, these advertisements are appealing to men who have no sexual partner of their own and want to enjoy some of the feel and the smell of a sexual relationship second-hand. But there are just as many men who *do* have sexual partners who enjoy the feel and the smell of their lover's underwear because it reminds them strongly of the woman who turns them on.

In *Sex Secrets of the Other Woman*, I described

how one woman slipped her soiled panties into her lover's briefcase so that he would discover them at work—a reminder of her sexuality that he could scarcely ignore. Although most of us have been brought up to think that intimate odors are distasteful, they can have a very strong aphrodisiac effect. During my research for this book, I talked to the young wife of an airline pilot from Santa Cruz, California, who regularly kept her panties on while urinating so that she could tuck them, still damp, into her husband's overnight bag.

That kind of total intimacy is the essence of frequent, active sex. And it's more than sex, too. It's a complete sharing of every part of your mind and your body with just one person—an absolute trust. If you're ready to give that trust and accept that trust, you can have a sexual relationship that transcends anything that you've ever imagined. You don't have to look for sexual fantasy in romantic novels. You don't have to dream that you're the heroine, having her bodice ripped open by the perfectly-profiled hero. You *are* the heroine. All the raw material that you need for a truly startling sex relationship is in your hands already, with your own partner; provided you're both willing to take the time to rediscover yourselves, and to explore all the varied experiences that sex has to offer.

One important rule is: talk first, act later. You shouldn't spring dramatic sexual surprises on your husband or lover. Although men love to read erotic fiction in which the voluptuous girl takes all the responsibility for the hero and heroine going to bed together, they almost always react badly to sexually assertive behavior from their own partners. It makes them feel as if they're no longer in charge—as if you've been secretly thinking that they're inadequate. Childish? Yes. Unreasonable? Yes. But that's the way most men are. For instance, they will love your erotic underwear, but they will love it even better if you show them the catalog before you order and say that you've been thinking about ordering some, and what would they like best? You don't necessarily have to buy exactly what they choose. But when you greet them at the door in your tasseled peephole bra and your tasseled open-crotch G-string, they'll feel that you're wearing it because *they* wanted you to wear it, and not because you're trying to perk up their flagging sexual performance.

I'll probably be accused of flagrant sexism, but in nearly a quarter-century of experience as a sex advisor, I've found that women are much more capable of turning around a faltering sexual relationship than men. Sometimes this means that women have to grit their teeth and abandon a great deal of their modesty and inhibitions. Sometimes it means that they have to provoke their partners sexually in ways they never dreamed they were capable. But, on the whole, women are far less sexually insecure, far less arrogant, and (when they understand the nature of their lover's desires) far more agreeable to try new sexual variations.

For instance, many women are quite happy to try minor acts of bondage. The experience of being sexually stimulated when you're quite helpless can be highly arousing . . . provided, of course, that the bondage isn't painful, and that you scrupulously observe the rules.

The rules being, of course, that you should never participate in bondage with somebody you don't already know and trust. You should never be left alone in a bondage situation. You should never be bound painfully or in any way that restricts your circulation. You should agree *before you begin any kind of bondage* that you will be immediately released, no questions asked, on a prearranged signal (especially important if you're going to be gagged or blindfolded). And on no account should any restriction be applied to your breathing.

Here's Jennie, twenty-nine, a schoolteacher from Sausalito, California, describing a bondage session with her live-in lover Frank: "We'd had a wonderful weekend. We'd shut away the world outside and spent the whole time together, drinking and listening to old records and making our own food, Italian, Chinese, steaks. By Sunday evening I was real tired, and I went to bed for a while. While I was sleeping, Frank came up and tied my wrists to the top of the bed with cord. He's a genius at knots. Well, naturally, since he was brought up on the ocean and always had a boat. He tied my ankles to the foot of the bed, too.

"I was wakened by a wet feeling between my legs. I opened my eyes and realized that Frank had lifted up my shirt (which was all I was wearing) and that he was licking my vagina. I tried to sit up, and then I realized that I couldn't move.

"At first I felt panic. I said, 'Frank, let me go!' I was afraid that I was suddenly discovering some weird new side to his personality that I'd never guessed at before. I felt incredibly vulnerable. Do you know what I mean? Incredibly defenseless. But all he did was smile at me and keep on licking me, and even though I struggled and twisted there was nothing I could do to get free.

"He was wearing nothing but jeans. But after a while he stopped licking me, and he stood up and took down his jeans and stood beside me naked, with his cock sticking out hard. I said, 'Are you going to untie me, or what?' He said no, he wasn't. He wasn't finished with me yet. He took his cock in his hand, and he pressed it against my breasts, and rolled it against my face. Then he pushed it up against my mouth. I wouldn't open my lips, but he said, 'If you don't suck my cock, I'll never let you go.'

"I guess it was then that I understood what the game was really all about. If I'd asked him, he would have let me go immediately. But it was, what? Kind of role-playing, you know? He was the slave-master and I was the slave. So I opened my mouth, and he pushed his cock right inside, right up against the roof of my mouth, so that I almost gagged. But it was very arousing, too. Not the kind of gagging when you feel sick. I sucked his cock really greedily, really hard. I love taking the whole of his cock-head into my mouth, just the glans, and then gently biting him just behind that ridge as if I'm going to bite the head of his cock off.

"I couldn't move my arms and I couldn't move my legs. I was a total prisoner with my mouth crammed full of cock. I think it was just about the most erotic thing that had ever happened to me.

"Anyway, I was sucking and licking at his cock, and then he suddenly took it out and said, 'That's it, forget it,' and he bent down and started licking my vagina again. I struggled. I didn't want him to do that just yet. But he kept on, and there was nothing I could do to stop him.

"He kept licking me and licking me until I was real close to coming, but then again he suddenly stopped and said 'forget it,' and went across and switched on the television and sat and watched some ridiculous nature program for about a quarter of an hour. I shouted and screamed at him for a while but he didn't take any notice. I felt like I was nothing at all, you know? Just something that he could use when he felt like it. But, when you think about it, that's the whole idea of bondage, isn't it? You're a slave, and it's a turn-on because you're totally helpless.

"After the nature program was finished, he came back and started touching my cunt with his fingers, rubbing my clitoris and sticking his fingers up me. Then he licked me again, with one finger up my cunt and another finger up my ass. I was relaxed by then, and he was really turning me on. I could feel myself starting to come. You know, like a thunderstorm grumbling in the distance. But then he stopped licking me and took out his fingers and started massaging my nipples instead. I was so close to an orgasm, I can't tell you! I could have screamed out loud!

"He massaged my breasts, and he teased my nipples. Then he kissed me again, and we had the fiercest, most passionate kissing session you can imagine. But again he stopped suddenly and presented his cock to my mouth, and said, 'Wet it, that's an order.'

"It sounds like he was being threatening, but he wasn't. Actually, he was just being demanding. I licked his cock until it was shiny with saliva, and he said, 'good.' Then he climbed on top of me, and pushed his cock right up inside my vagina, and he fucked me like he's never fucked me before. Beautiful! Strong, long strokes. His whole body working, his ass tight. And I couldn't do anything but lay there spread-eagled on the bed helpless while he fucked and fucked and fucked.

"Never in the whole time that we'd been together had I reached an orgasm just by fucking. But I did then. And of course, I couldn't move. I was all tied up! I shook that bed until it rattled. I thought I shouted out loud, but Tony told me afterward that I didn't. And that was the first time that I'd ever come first; so even when I was finished, Tony was still fucking me, and that feeling was so incredible, I didn't know whether I liked it or I hated it. I didn't know if I could stand it! But I *had* to stand it because I was tied up, and he went on and on and then he came; and I know that it was terrific for him, because he practically blacked out, and then he lay down on top of me, and he kissed me, and he said, 'I'm sorry, I'm sorry.'

"I said, 'Why are you saying you're sorry? That was amazing.' But he kept on saying he was sorry, and I guess that was part of it. He needed to dominate me, and I liked him dominating me, but at the same time we were equal partners, and he didn't want me to think that he was going to treat me like a slave the whole time. We both came out of that experience feeling that we'd done something exciting and daring and loving each other all the more."

I talked with several men and women who were interested in the erotic properties of rubber . . . it's smell, its cling, and the sweatiness it induced. They had bought a variety of rubber garments, including so-called "dance briefs" which featured erect rubber dildos molded on to their insides so that a woman could walk around all day in clinging latex panties with a large rubber penis buried in her vagina and a smaller rubber penis in her anus. "Athletic briefs" for men had a sheath for the penis in front, and a rubber dildo to penetrate the anus in the back.

In some cases, rubber enthusiasts *have* to be dressed in rubber in order to achieve sexual satisfaction, but most of those couples I spoke to who were "rubber fans" used these specialist garments simply to arouse themselves, in the same way that they might have used sexy underwear or sex-toys.

Since I raised the topic in earlier books, I have

had scores of enquiries about "wet sex," especially by couples who have tried it, and enjoyed it, but now feel guilty or embarrassed or worried about it. Some are worried that they enjoyed it too much.

"Wet sex" is the generic description for any kind of sex play which involves urination. The eroticism of wet sex is undoubtedly childish—it's "dirty" and it's "naughty" and it's "rude." But that doesn't mean that it can't be an exciting form of love-play for adults; any more than building model railroads can't be an exciting recreation for children over the age of twenty-one.

Many couples derive erotic pleasure from watching each other urinate—some from urinating over each other or even drinking each other's urine. Since urine is sterile there is no harm in swallowing a very small amount. Many explorers and pioneers have survived in the desert by drinking urine, without any catastrophic ill-effects.

Here's Geoff, a thirty-three-year-old geophysicist, from Butte, Montana: "I don't know why, but the sight and the sound of my wife Sophie sitting on the john always used to turn me on. She didn't mind if I came into the bathroom when she was peeing and talked to her. So one day I plucked up the nerve to say, 'Let me see,' when she was taking a pee. She's pretty broad-minded, she wasn't embarrassed. She opened her legs, and I could see the pee jetting out of her—and, I don't know, maybe it sounds perverted or something, but it was beautiful. That beautiful cunt, wide open, and this thin shining stream coming out.

"A couple of evenings later, when she was just about to take a bath, I came into the bathroom, and Sophie was taking off her eyelashes. When she sat on the john, I said, 'Let me touch you.' She didn't understand at first. She said, 'I'm having a pee, do you mind?' But I said, 'Let me touch you while you pee.'

"I could tell that she didn't really want to do it. I could tell. But when she started to pee I put my hand down between her legs and slid my index finger up into her cunt, and she let loose this hot stream right into the palm of my hand. I finger-fucked her while she peed, and when she'd finished I massaged her wet cunt, and both of us were totally turned on.

"She climbed into the tub, and she said, 'Come on, you too,' and I climbed into the tub along with her. She lay back, and I was kneeling astride her, and she took hold of my cock and said, 'Come on, I've peed for you. You pee for me.'

"You don't know how hard it is to pee to order, especially when you're turned on, and your cock's as hard as a bone. But the feeling is quite sensational, when it does spurt out. I peed in jets, one long jet after another, and Sophie took hold of my cock and guided those jets into her face, into her mouth, over her breasts. Then we fucked, in the bath, not very successfully, because fucking in the bath is one of the most difficult things that two human beings can ever try to do. But we both felt that we'd broken down a barrier. We felt that we weren't ashamed or embarrassed about *anything* any more."

Bob and Christine, both thirty-two, from Portland, Oregon, reported that they occasionally enjoyed a "wet sex picnic." Christine wrote, "We regularly spend weekends in the woods, walking and picnicking. One afternoon about six or seven months ago we were walking back to our camper when we started talking about one of our neighbors, who always makes us laugh. I laughed so hard that I started to wet myself. I lifted up my skirt so that I wouldn't wet it, but I didn't have time to do anything else but pee right through my panties.

"But immediately, Bob came up and he put his hand between my legs, and he said, 'That was one of the sexiest things I ever saw.' And he rolled down my wet panties, and he unzipped his fly, and we had sex right there, right up against a mossy old tree.

"The next time we went out for a walk in the woods, I said to him, 'I have to pee . . . do you want me to do it the same way I did before?' Bob said 'Sure.' So I tied my skirt up around my waist, and I stood right next to him, and I just let myself go. I was only wearing these little white nylon panties, so it went straight through, and ran down my legs, all warm and streaming. Then Bob took out his cock and slipped it into the front of my panties and peed right up against my cunt. It was a real hot gush, and I'd never felt anything like that before. We laid down our bedroll, and we took off all our clothes and made love naked, with the sun shining and the birds singing, and we felt like Adam and Eve."

Whatever the delights of spontaneous sex, you will have to make a certain amount of plans if you intend to make love almost every night of the week. You will have to think about varying the locations for your lovemaking (like Bob and Christine, planning their walks in the woods); about what you might wear (if anything); and whether you want to indulge any particular fantasy that you or your lover have been harboring.

Making love in the open air can vary from the picturesque to the raunchy. Leonard and Marion, a young couple from Glendale, California, regularly enjoy lovemaking in their new Buick . . . even though it's parked in the driveway. They do it at night "and the windows pretty soon steam up," but all the same there's the added frisson that their neighbors might come past and catch them at it.

Lucy, a twenty-three-year-old newlywed from New Rochelle, New York, occasionally takes the train into Manhattan so that she can visit her lawyer husband David at work. "I never wear anything underneath my dress, and I take him into the stationery closet and take my dress off and suck his cock for him; or else we try to make love on a chair."

Winston and Maria, however, an unmarried couple from White Plains, New York, enjoy driving into the Connecticut woods with a bottle of champagne and a blanket, and making love in the open. "There's nothing like feeling the breeze on your bare skin, nothing."

You and your lover can be making love almost every night provided you're both prepared to put a little thought and caring into your sexual relationship. Maj-Britt Bergstrom-Walan, one of Sweden's leading sex therapists, once told me, "It's extraordinary that a man will lavish more time on cleaning his car at the weekend than he will on making love to his wife. He will discuss his car happily for hours. He will discuss his career happily for hours. But when it comes to sex, his mouth is sealed."

Sex is one of the most exciting and rewarding of human experiences, and it's a condemnation of our moral attitudes that, even today, so many people remain inhibited and ill-informed about it. Even today, I still talk to women who regard sex as a duty rather than a pleasure, and are quite astonished when they discover that they, too, are actually supposed to be enjoying it. "I thought it was something that men liked and women just had to put up with it."

I still talk to men who never consider their partner's sexual feelings and have no regard for their sexual satisfaction. "Women don't need it the same way men do. Anyway, she never complains."

Because of attitudes like this, both men and women are missing out on hours of intimate pleasure and failing to enjoy the well-being and closeness that good and frequent lovemaking can offer.

Mutual knowledge comes first: which is why I have developed the Mutual Discovery Session. If you find it difficult to suggest to your partner that you try it, simply let him or her read this book, and see for him- or herself the sexual pleasures that you can open up for yourselves.

When a couple are able to share everything they feel and think about sex, without being anxious that their partner will consider them perverted or dirty-minded, they can create a physical and emotional relationship between them that enhances their life in almost every aspect. Sexually contented people are more capable at work, more even-minded in a crisis, and (if recent medical statistics can be trusted) can expect to live longer.

Your *target* for lovemaking should be six days a week; and even if you're both tired, you should try to make some kind of sexually affectionate gesture, every single day. It doesn't necessarily have to lead to anything. It can be nothing more than an intimate caress while you're watching television in bed; or a gentle kissing of your breasts; or a slow, gourmet kissing of each other's genitals.

The important thing is to keep up the habit of showing each other that you are sexually attracted; that the fire of erotic passion that brought you together has never gone out; and never will. Sexual relationships are like anything else worthwhile: the more you put into them, the more you get back out.

Ella, a twenty-three-year-old grade-school teacher from Los Angeles, agreed to try out the six-days-a-week sex plan with her live-in lover Sam, a thirty-two-year-old civil engineer. First of all they went through the Mutual Discovery Session—then they planned out a month of daily activities which would keep them sexually active six days a week.

Here's Ella's own (uncensored) diary of her first week:

MONDAY: We'd agreed to try the Mutual Discovery Session and then to start making love six days a week, but frankly we were both pretty skeptical. After all, we had a terrific sex relationship already and we didn't think that any kind of 'plan' was going to improve it. But all the same we said okay and agreed to start on President's Day because that was a holiday for both of us. We were asked to bring along anything that we thought might turn us on—even if our partners didn't know about it. The only thing that's ever turned me on, apart from Sam and some of the boyfriends I've had before, is a porno movie called *Debbie Does Dallas*, so I got hold of a video of that.

We followed the Mutual Discovery Session to the letter. We laughed a lot when we were showering together, but all the same we enjoyed it. Afterwards we lay on the bed, naked, and poured some champagne (supplied free of charge, thank you!) and played some really sappy Roberta Flack records which we both like—*The First Time Ever I Saw Your Face*, stuff like that.

I started by exploring Sam's body according to instructions! I kept laughing to start with, but after a while I realized that I was learning things about him that I'd never known before, and he was, too. I found out that he loved me sucking his nipples, but that he couldn't bear me to bite them; and the only reason he hadn't complained about it before was because he hadn't wanted to spoil the moment.

Of course my favorite part was exploring his cock. To tell you the truth, I'd never liked the idea of kissing or sucking a man's cock, in fact I'd never done it to Sam properly, only quickly, and the main reason for that was I thought I might hurt him or I might do it wrong. I didn't realize until then (when he came out straight and told me) that he was absolutely aching for me to suck his cock. So I did it, very slowly, taking my time, without feeling rushed, because this was a proper discovery session, rather than normal lovemaking.

More than anything else, what I enjoyed about the Mutual Discovery Session was that there was no hurry. And there was no assumption that either of us knew all about making love, which we obviously didn't. There were quite small things—like how to massage a man's balls, or how to turn him on by sliding your finger up his ass and pressing against his prostrate gland—I'd never known any of that before. It's not the kind of thing your mom tells you, and you sure don't learn it in school.

What I liked most about sucking Sam's cock was running the head of it from side to side across my lips, and then sucking out the juice. I hadn't realized that men produce so much lubricant, and it tastes incredible. Subtle, but incredible.

I also hadn't known anything at all about anal penetration. I didn't know you could do it; and I certainly hadn't known *how* to do it. For me, that was one of the most instructive parts of the whole session.

When Sam got around to exploring me, I was amazed at what I didn't know about my own body and my own responses. What also amazed me was how much I hadn't told him about myself and what

I liked (and what I didn't like). He had always been much too quick and rough when he was making love to me. Most often, I didn't quite reach a climax at all. But he hadn't understood that it was his obligation to make sure that I reached a climax if I wanted to; and I hadn't understood how to encourage him to do it.

I *did* know that I peed from my urethra, rather than my vagina. After all, I'm a school teacher! But it's quite obvious that plenty of girls that I teach are woefully ignorant about their bodies, and about sex. Some of them are making love to boys at the age of thirteen or fourteen, and just because some irresponsible kid has stuck himself inside them they think they know it all. In fact, the ignorance about sex that I meet in the classroom is horrific; and it shows that parents are either too embarrassed to tell their kids what's what, or else they simply don't know. And these parents are the kids who were growing up during the so-called 'permissive era!'

For the first time I showed Sam how to caress my clitoris so that he could arouse me quickly and gently. After that, he felt like an expert! He explored inside my vagina, and that was another first. In fact that changed *both* of our attitudes. Like most women, I'd always thought of my vagina as something negative, a hole. After all, when you're a little kid, boys turn around and say 'Look at you, you haven't got one,' and it's easy to keep on feeling that you've got something missing.

Just because your vagina is inside you, that doesn't mean it isn't just as active and positive as a penis . . . and finding out about that really made me feel more sexually confident and better about my whole body. It changed my attitude toward lovemaking, too.

Again, nobody had ever penetrated my anus, and

when Sam started to push his fingers up me I really went tight, and practically squeezed his fingers off with my muscles! But we both took our time, and I learned how to relax. I found the best position was for me to kneel on the bed with my head on the pillow and my bottom in the air, holding the cheeks of my bottom wide apart with my own fingers. Then Sam could explore my ass really deeply and easily. I have to admit that I didn't like the feeling of it at all, not at first. But after a while I began to like it. It gave me a really weird sexual sensation that I'd never felt before, as if I was opening up my whole body.

Well, when we finished that Mutual Discovery Session it was dark, and we realized that we'd been touching and caressing and exploring each other for nearly three hours! We made love, very simply and very slowly, and that was a perfect end to a day of amazing revelation. I started off a cynic, I ended up a total convert. I'd recommend an afternoon of mutual exploration like that to any couple, whether they're married or living together, whether they think they're brilliant at sex or not. The things you can learn! The things you can tell your partner, too!

I learned for instance that Sam has always been dying for me to shave my pubic hair. He had never said a word, before then. Not a word! I wasn't sure that I wanted to do it, not all the time, but I agreed to try it for a while. And I told him that I'd always wanted to make love on the seashore. It was always something I'd dreamed of.

I guess the greatest thing that the Mutual Discovery Session did for us was to make us both realize that we didn't know everything about each other; and it stopped us from taking each other for granted. We also learned that many of the sexual acts that we had always thought of as perverted or dirty were sexual acts that millions of people do every day; and that so long as nobody gets hurt or emotionally dominated, then just about anything goes.

TUESDAY: Before Sam came home, I did what he wanted, and showered, and shaved off my pubic hair. It's blonde and quite fine, so it wasn't difficult, but I think I might have to use a depilatory to keep it smooth. Actually, I thought I wouldn't like it, but looking at myself in the mirror I thought I looked extremely feminine—and after all, those young girls on the beach in their high-cut bathing costumes must do the same. Can't start being an old maid at twenty-three! I wore a blue short-sleeved sweat-shirt, a very short cream pleated tennis-skirt, and white sox, but no panties. I was so excited at the prospect of Sam coming home that my vagina was wet even before he turned his key in the lock. But I don't suppose that's going to happen *every* day!

When he arrived home, he'd brought me flowers. The first time in just about a century! We kissed like crazy. In fact we both acted like kids on our first date. We'd both planned to wait for sex until after dinner, but this *was* our first day, and we couldn't resist it. I knelt down in front of him and tugged down his zipper. Then I wrestled his cock out of his shorts, and it was hard and hot and it was practically steaming. I had it halfway down my throat before Sam could say anything, and he was still holding his flowers!

I sucked him and rubbed him, and then I lay back on the living-room rug and lifted my tennis-skirt. That was it as far as Sam was concerned! He took one look at my shaved cunt, and he was out of his shirt and out of his pants, and he was kneeling between my thighs with his cock in his hand. He pushed it up me very slowly; and for the first time we both watched it go in, and we made love as slowly and as luxuriously as we could manage.

Sam came first. I squeezed my vagina tight, and I could feel his cock pulsing as he squirted out his sperm. I took out his cock with my hand and kept rubbing it and massaging it while it slowly went soft. It was wonderfully wet. But then I said, 'Come on, I showed you how to lick me. I need to come.'

I think that was the first time he understood that he really did have a responsibility to make sex as satisfying for me as it was for him. But he didn't complain. He turned around, in the 'sixty-nine' position, and he started to flick my clitoris with the tip of his tongue, in just the way I'd showed him how.

It was good for me, too, because I could open my mouth and suck at his soft cock and his balls. They were smothered in sperm and cunt juice, and they tasted like Sam and me, all mixed together, which is what we were. When I opened my mouth really wide, I could take in practically all of his cock and most of his balls, even though it almost choked me. I was right on the verge of having a climax, and his cock started to go stiff again, so I had to take it out.

We made love for a second time about three o'clock in the morning; but we were both very tired and satisfied, so it didn't amount to very much more than a lazy fuck.

WEDNESDAY: Sam was obviously determined to pay me back for the way that I'd turned him on yesterday, so he surprised me by coming home early. He'd brought me a package, all wrapped up in glossy silver paper. When I opened it, it turned out to be a plastic penis with a vibrating motor in it!

I wasn't too happy about using something artificial, but Sam said that we'd promised to try anything and everything, without question, so there was nothing I could do. I was amazed that he wanted to see me with a plastic penis up my cunt, but he said, 'Wait till you've tried it.'

We did actually manage to wait until after we'd had a club sandwich and a couple of glasses of wine. After last night, we weren't all that urgent to go to bed together. But then Sam went through to the bedroom and undressed and lay naked on the bed, and I came to join him.

He kissed me, and then he fondled and kissed my breasts. He really took his time; and I was almost impatient for him to start with the plastic penis. But at last he ran his hands down between my thighs and stroked my cunt, and even though I'd promised myself that I wouldn't respond so quickly, I couldn't help it. It's a fantastic feeling to know that a man wants you so much.

He picked up the plastic penis and placed the head of it between my legs. He said, 'Watch, it's terrific.' It was almost like watching your own porno movie, with my bare-shaved cunt really stretched wide open and this pink plastic penis sliding in and out of me. I was determined that I was going to hate it—that it was just like jerking yourself off. But when your lover does it for you, somehow that's different. He stroked my forehead and caressed my breasts, and all the time this plastic penis kept urging itself in and out of me.

It took me a long time to reach an orgasm. At least it felt like a long time. Maybe ten, maybe twenty minutes? But when it began, I knew that I didn't want Sam to stop. I also knew that as soon as I'd climaxed he'd fuck me with his own cock, and the thought of that made me feel doubly sexy.

I climaxed so violently that I thought it was going to break my back. But while I was still in spasm,

Sam started fucking me with these really long, quick, fluid strokes.

I've heard about multiple orgasms, and I suppose that was what I had. It just went on and on, and I could hardly breathe. All I could think about was this cock that kept pushing itself into me; and hoping that Sam would come; and at the same time praying that he wouldn't.

When he did, he took his cock out of me, and held it in his hand, and shot his sperm all over my breasts, all over my stomach, all over the bed. It was like we'd both been sexually liberated, we could do whatever we felt like, and it was wonderful.

THURSDAY: We were both tired. I'd had a long day taking my class to the zoo; Sam had had a long day at the office, making up for coming home early yesterday. But after supper, we bathed together, and lay in bed naked watching television, and Sam reached around me and slowly massaged my clitoris. He did it in just the nice way that I'd shown him but using hardly any pressure at all . . . and so slow that I was quietly turned on without feeling that we had to have a major confrontational fuck.

FRIDAY: Was very different than Thursday. We were both well-rested. It was the end of the week, and after work Sam took me to one of my favorite restaurants overlooking the ocean. When we got home, he ran us a deep hot bath with some new bath-oil that he'd bought, and we both climbed into the tub.

He soaped me all over, my neck, my breasts, my stomach, between my legs. We kissed and fondled in the bath. Then he helped me out and toweled me dry; and treated me like a queen. He carried me into the bedroom and laid me on the bed and said, 'You don't have to do anything, anything at all.' He put on a sexy video on the television and brought me a glass of champagne, and then he knelt down between my legs and he started to lick my cunt.

It was paradise. I didn't have to do anything but lie back and let it all wash over me. He took his time—first of all flicking my clitoris with the tip of his tongue so that I began to get turned on, then dipping his tongue into my vagina, to moisten it, then back again on my clitoris.

I didn't have an orgasm. After five or ten minutes I needed him to make love to me. I took hold of his shoulders and pulled at him and said, 'Fuck me, for goodness sake. I can't take any more.'

He was good, and slow, and deep. He was really good. I wouldn't have believed he was the same guy from a week ago. He wanted to please me, he took pride in turning me on; and he did. He came, and lay on top of me; and I didn't need an orgasm right then, all I needed was to hold this man who cared so much about what I felt, and about what I needed, and that was plenty.

Later on, though, when he was asleep, I dipped my fingers down between my legs, so that my fingers were covered in his sperm, and I sucked them; and I could taste him then, and that was more than satisfaction enough.

SATURDAY: We spent with friends at a barbecue. Everybody commented that Sam and I seemed different somehow. My friend Vera said that we seemed so much closer, like young love or something! And I guess, yes, that's what it was. When we got home that evening, Sam said, 'Let's take the night off . . . I'm bushed. We only have to do it six nights a week, don't we?'

But I wasn't going to let him get away with that.

I had a special surprise for him. I'd bought a black lace bra with holes in the front for my nipples to peep through, and a split-crotch G-string so that the lips of my cunt showed through the lace, and fishnet stockings, and a garter belt. I waited until Sam was in bed with his glass of wine and his book, and then I appeared in the doorway and said, 'Ta-da! Cabaret time!'

I don't know where Sam found the energy, but that night he fucked me twice. I was still wearing that underwear in the morning, and when he woke up, he fucked me again. Sexually . . . the best week ever! And there's still next week to look forward to!

9

A Month of Love

Now, your sex life is in your own hands. The pleasures of six-days-a-week sex are there, waiting for you to enjoy them. But as a final suggestion, here's a diary of sixty-six erotic things you can do during your first month of love.

Week One:

Monday: Day one . . . and time for your Mutual Discovery Session. Explore each other's bodies and each other's sexual responses.
Tuesday: Encourage you lover to stimulate your clitoris with his tongue until you have an orgasm.
Wednesday: Greet your lover naked when he returns home, and make love to him before he has the chance to undress.
Thursday: Insist that your lover give you three orgasms in one evening.
Friday: Don't allow your lover to have intercourse with you until you've given him fifteen minutes of teasing oral sex.
Saturday: Dress up in erotic underwear, and take your lover to bed.

Week Two:

Monday: Good grooming day . . . change your

hairstyle, polish your nails, wax your legs, shave your pubic hair.

Tuesday: Buy yourselves some sex-toys . . . both vaginal vibrators and anal stimulators.

Wednesday: Play out one of your favorite erotic fantasies when you go to bed.

Thursday: Give your lover a massage with professional massage-oil, finishing up by masturbating him until he ejaculates.

Friday: Buy a bottle of champagne, put it on ice, and wait for him naked in bed.

Saturday: Take a trip to the country, and make love in the open air. Spend as long as you can naked in the great outdoors. But watch out for game wardens!

Week Three:

Monday: Encourage your lover to stimulate you anally . . . with fingers and tongue and sex-toys. See if he can penetrate your anus with his (well-lubricated) penis.

Tuesday: Hold each other closely and affectionately in bed, and spend five minutes (no more) caressing each other's genitals with mouth and tongue. But don't worry about reaching climaxes unless you really feel the urge.

Wednesday: Try a little bondage. Have your lover tie your arms and your feet, and stimulate you however he wants to . . . always remembering the rules!

Thursday: Good grooming day for your lover. Bathe him, wash his hair, clip his nails, shave his pubic hair if a naked penis appeals to you.

Friday: Rent or buy some sexy videos, and spend the evening in bed together trying to concentrate on the action.

Saturday: Stay naked all day, and kiss and caress each other whenever possible.

Week Four:

Monday: Play the truth game . . . ask each other if there are any secret sexual desires which you still haven't been able to divulge . . . and then tell the truth.

Tuesday: Play hookey from work, both of you, and spend the afternoon at a strange motel under the name of 'Mr. and Mrs. D. Juan,' making love.

Wednesday: Treat each other to an evening of romance, playing romantic records and touching each other intimately.

Thursday: Be dominant with your lover. Demand that he takes you to bed, and penetrate him anally with finger or vibrator while he's making love to you. No protests allowed!

Friday: Give him an evening of oral sex . . . all he has to do is lie back while you suck him.

Saturday: Dress up, go out together, and behave like the close, harmonious, sexy couple you are. Dine, dance, and then come home together and hold each other close and think how lucky you are that you found each other.